STUPID ENOUGH

to

SUCCEED

The Millennial Entrepreneur's Guide
to Achieving Business Hypergrowth

JEFF NAEEM

AuthorHouse™
1663 Liberty Drive
Bloomington, IN 47403
www.authorhouse.com
Phone: 1 (800) 839-8640

Published by AuthorHouse 07/28/2017

ISBN: 978-1-5246-9939-0 (sc)
ISBN: 978-1-5246-9938-3 (e)

Library of Congress Control Number: 2017911022

Print information available on the last page.

"A fun and insightful book on how a millennial launched and grew a successful business – with lots of hard-earned lessons."

—*Verne Harnish, author Scaling Up (Rockefeller Habits 2.0) and founder Entrepreneurs' Organization (EO)*

"*Stupid Enough to Succeed* tells the true story of entrepreneurship, It means falling down ten times and getting up eleven, it means shirking better judgment and common sense to pursue crazy ideas...some of which actually work."

—*Bruce Eckfeldt, Inc. 500 CEO, Writer for Inc.com, Certified Gazelles Coach*

"*Stupid Enough to Succeed* is everything but stupid. It is smart, entertaining, real, practical advice to get your business up and off the ground successfully."

—*Mike Michalowicz, author of Profit First*

"Get up, decide what to do and do it. If your dream is to build something or provide a service that people will pay for, you'll put yourself ahead of everyone else by reading - and applying - the advice in this book."

—*Jason W. Womack MEd, MA, Author and Cofounder of GetMomentum.com*

"In my coaching practice I always emphasize tenacious tactical execution. *Stupid Enough to Succeed* is all about how to implement great ideas and I heartily recommend that budding entrepreneurs read it and consider Jeff's advice."

— *Dave Schoenbeck Business & Executive Coach and former SVP at Babies "R" Us.*

"*Stupid Enough to Succeed* is a must read for any entrepreneur thinking about starting his or her own business or to grow their business. Jeff's hands-on style comes through as he shares the real life ups and downs of being an entrepreneur."

—*Jack Killion, Serial Entrepreneur & Author of Network All the Time, Everywhere, with Everybody*

"This book should be called 'The Real-Deal to Starting a Business' because that is exactly what it is. This is the most accurate account I have ever seen in print about what the startup experience is really like for everyday entrepreneurs. Reading this book will save you time and money if you take heed. (Definitely not stupid!)"

—*Jill Johnson, CEO, Institute for Entrepreneurial Leadership*

Contents

Dedication

This book is dedicated to every kid who had a lemonade stand, who mowed lawns or washed cars, for you are the future captains of industry.

Acknowledgments

None of us can ever succeed all on our own. That old saying, "No man is an island" rings so true for those of us that chose the entrepreneurial journey. I would be shamefully remiss if I didn't thank all those who helped me along the way—you know; the ones that made me smarter. So, where do I begin?

With my parents, of course. First, a thousand thanks to my father, Dr. Sheikh Naeem for imparting his unwavering drive, and for always remaining a source of inspiration. And for mom, Maria Naeem, for her constant support and for her everlasting sense of humor. I guess that's where I got mine from. To my siblings, Joe—who may have first sparked the intellectual bug in me; Mike, for coming on board when we needed the help; Marissa, for her encouragement. I can't help but thank grandma for running all those lemonade pitchers down all those years. (Read the book and you'll know why!) Thanks grandpa for first teaching me how to work with my hands and always being so supportive as I grew my business.

I have to give a special shout-out to Chris Lipper, my dedicated facilitator from The Alternative Board®, for: always giving me a hard time to move me forward; for always pushing me to get to the next level; for always ensuring that I focus on my vision. Thanks, Chris. Your efforts definitely paid off!

You would not be reading this book if not for my editor Barry Cohen; thanks for the Vulcan Mind Meld—the countless hours of pulling all this stuff out of my head. Yay! We got it done.

Okay, so let's take a step back in time. I owe a special thanks to Hamilton College philosophy professor Bob Simon for teaching me critical thinking. And, to my college advisor, Professor Jay Williams, for reminding me that your work should always be one that includes big picture thinking— and always doing what you love. Don't let practicality spoil your adventure!

Harkening back to my brief adventure in corporate America—my suit days, I thank my Northwestern Mutual mentors Ryan Bass, Kevin Stein and Ben Deng for helping me get my sales game to the next level. I'm really more comfortable without the tie these days. Then there were my early sales teachers, affectionately, the Cutco Crew. Thanks for believing in me. Dennis Jankowski—thanks for opening the door to my sales and business career, and Do'oa Yassin-Holloway for being one of my first mentors.

I need to go back just a little further. Thanks to my high school teachers, Dr. David Donovan, one of the first to contribute to my passion for lifelong learning; Mr. Rosenhaus, for helping me get into my first choice college and always having a sense of humor as I made him fill out yet another application...sixteen and counting.

It was you, Dan Nugent—thanks for telling me to hang up my suit and tie and go haul junk. Who would have thought that a casual suggestion on the way to the bar would turn into an entire enterprise? And thanks to all my entrepreneurial heroes: Richard Branson, Tim Ferris, Steve Jobs, Tony Hsieh, Seth Godin, Michael Gerber and many others who inspired me to become an entrepreneur and stick it out through the good and the bad.

—*Jeff Naeem*

Foreword

Wherever you are on your entrepreneurial
   journey—
just thinking about going into business, just
   starting
your business or putting out the many
   fires you
encounter from day to day, this book will
   help you
start up and ramp up your business faster
   and better.

Stupid Enough to Succeed tells the true
story of entrepreneurship. Jeff doesn't try
to convince you what a gifted leader he is or
how brilliant his business strategy has been.
Instead, he tells you about the multitude of
slap-your-forehead mistakes he's made and
WTF situations he's found himself in.

Through his honesty and vulnerability,
you learn what it really means to be an
entrepreneur. It means falling down ten

times and getting up eleven, it means not making the same mistake twice, but finding new ones to make, and it means shirking better judgment and common sense to pursue crazy ideas...some of which actually work out.

So, just dive in and prepare to make some of your own mistakes—as long as you're willing to learn from them.

Bruce Eckfelt
Inc 500 CEO, Writer for Inc.com, Certified
Gazelles Coach

From the Editor's Desk...

This book focuses on entrepreneurship, leadership and youth development. Simply stated, the author's thesis on successful entrepreneurship reads like this:

"Start your business early, when you are young, unencumbered and more willing and able to take risks. Why? Because you have less to lose and less craving for stability. The experience will teach you about money management and financial literacy, as well as the skills to run a business day-to-day."

So, how is this book different from the rest? This book gives the reader a youthful perspective and is "anti-millennial"— it portrays young adults that are the complete opposite of the stereotype, with an emphasis on a strong work ethic. It also comes from an unconventional place, based on the author's experience in a low-tech industry.

There are several important reader take-aways. To wit, in the author's own words: "The fun and the passion comes from the experience of creating and running a business itself—not necessarily from the specific business". This book will help you understand the implications of bootstrapping versus using Other People's Money (keeping the equity). It is vitally important to understand and recognize that a hobby does not equal a business. You must know what the market demand is; you must keep educating yourself and study things that will help you think critically. Unless the business is largely automated, it demands full attention in the early stages—it should not be a part-time effort.

Most important, here's how the reader will benefit from the author's knowledge: by avoiding costly mistakes, by getting started sooner and from the author's proven game plan/track record of success.

So, what influenced the author to develop his theory/thesis? He was a kidpreneur, selling wrapping paper door-to-door at the age of 7. Early habits yielded early lessons—positive ones. He derived much of his influence from his father, who was success-driven—an immigrant who became a cardiologist. In addition, he began his business with a partner, rather than alone, providing a safety net. Finally, he studied what didn't work in traditional legacy companies, and focused on the new generation of maverick entrepreneurs' success methods.

—*Barry Cohen*

"Ever Tried. Ever Failed. No Matter. Try Again. Fail Again. Fail Better."

—*Samuel Beckett*

Introduction

"When You Stop Doing Things for Fun You Might as Well be Dead."

—*Ernest Hemingway*

So, here's what you can expect to find between the covers of this book. It's all about the "why" for us youthpreneurs. We are redefining what makes business succeed today. We are creating companies that are more nimble; we are taking on and BEATING THE BIG GUYS! So, let's pop the hood and find out why. Oh, and you may be wondering about the title.

So, what's with this "stupid" business? Well, yes, my tongue got stuck in my cheek. From time to time, we'll show you both the stupid and the not so stupid things we ourselves—and others, have done in business.

Stupid Enough to Succeed is our Millennial generation's new creed for a different approach to business. Simply put, it's about failing our way to the top. The days of overwrought spreadsheets and stuffy boardroom presentations are over. The age of action is here.

There are some distinct advantages to youth. We have more time ahead of us to try, to fail, to learn and to succeed. So, why is it good to start when you're young, naïve and this side of slightly crazy? Apple founder Steve Jobs said, "Stay hungry, stay foolish". Yes, we are brash, impulsive, often imprudent and we succeed in spite of ourselves. We make it up as we go along. Let's disassemble it for you. This is how we millennials create and run businesses.

Jeff's Lesson # 1: (Not Stupid) Start your business before you have too many obligations. Do it before people are counting on you and it's only yourself that you're risking. If the ship has already sailed on that front, then it's just a matter of mitigating the risk where you can. Make sure your wife/husband is supportive and/or can still reasonably cover the bills, or get to a point where you can be in that position. Because there are 5 million challenges to being an entrepreneur; having an angry spouse and unfed kids is not one you want to worry about. Generations ago this would have been less likely with more traditional gender roles and a single income household.

"When You Got Nothing, You've Got Nothing to Lose."
—Bob Dylan

Jeff's Lesson #2: (Also Not Stupid) No plan B. A seasoned entrepreneur from a different generation approached me and asked, "What's your plan B?" I told him there is No plan B. Plan B is planning to fail. Now look, if what you're working on is some highly risky invention where it's impossible to even do any substantial market research, then that's one thing. But for the majority of businesses you have to jump in and not look back. Another great way to put it is the "burn your ships" analogy. Simply stated, that means you close every door behind you so there is no avenue of retreat.

Jeff's Lesson #3: (Usually Not Stupid) Make it up as you go along—an "on the job MBA". I was always against business school. It doesn't have to be perfect; just get it out – we'll get it out there and fix it as we go. Pivot as needed. Twitter had a HUGE pivot. And that's okay because at least you're doing stuff, moving the ball forward. I always thought business school was a waste of time. I bought the books that I wanted to read and educated myself through the key areas. You don't have to spend hundreds of thousands of dollars for information that's readily available online. Does it help to have someone holding your hand? Sure, but if you need that then you probably shouldn't be an entrepreneur.

Jeff's Lesson # 4: (Definitely Not Stupid) Form Your Own Advisory Board. Don't pay exorbitant sums to hear a text book repeated back to you. Guys, girls, kids—it's action over theory. Jump right in; theory is a great way to delay action. "The supreme misfortune is when theory outstrips performance" - Leonardo Da Vinci. As a generation, we have unique qualities. We view the world and/or our careers and business differently. We welcome and embrace challenge, not retreat from it. We invite it so we can tame it, harness it and conquer it. We manage ourselves and others differently. We'll talk about that more later in this book.

Jeff's Lesson # 5: (Way Beyond Stupid) Do the unconventional by going down your OWN path. In college I studied philsophy with a double minor in world religions and photography. Why? I learned to think critically. And I confess, I did enjoy it along the way. Here's one they probably won't tell you in ivy league business school: make friends with competitors. At first glance, this may actually be one of the oldest pieces of advice when it comes to business/leadership, which as Francis Ford Coppolla wrote in Godfather II, "Keep your friends close but your enemies closer." If you're friends with your competition then you can have less fear over underhanded anti-competitive practices. But even better, my best referral sources are people who do things very similar to what we do but not exactly the same, or in the same area. I frequently cross refer business with other junk removal companies who simply don't service certain parts of our territory and vice versa. Additionally, I have had major luck cross referring business to movers and professional organizers who both do similar work to us, but just different enough for us to regularly encounter requests for each other's services. Instead, we all just get to hand off the work we don't specialize in and do the work we do excel at.

So, here's the big question. I told you it's all about the "why." WHY are we as a generation of millennial entrepreneurs going in this direction? *Because the other stuff didn't work.* Legacy institutions and methods failed us. How did they fail us and why? They created waste, pollution and stagnation. Large bureautcratic institutions were slow to change and failed to pivot. Just look at Nokia®, Blackberry® and Kodak®. The world is full of graveyards of slow to change companies.

Why else do we feel the need to reinvent the wheel? Because we're sick of the MAN. We've come to the realization that your work doesn't have to be some drudgery with a constant lack of satisfaction and fulfillment. We don't have to slave at a career we don't like. Because we're less concerned with having a really nice car and a mc mansion – instead, we want and need job satisfaction – which in corporate America can be tough. But, by becoming entrepreneurs or working at more forward thinking and progressive companies, we can have that. More progressive companies are often letting entrepreneurs become more entrepreneurial WITHIN the organization—which benefits the management, too. Because it fosters innovation, there is a legitimate revenue based justification as well.

One area where we definitely differ from past generations of business owners: management is different – it's more particpatory and more empowering. We'll discuss more on this later in the book. A true mark of today's businesses involves the level of employee engagement—a direct result of passion. For example, at Apple®, the original team was way ahead of its time. The product developers had T-shirts that read "80 hours a week and loving it"—and they wore them with pride. In the past, it became necessary to pass laws against working such hours. At one point it might have been considered a crime to make people work that many hours, but now, because of more passion driven engaging work, people are not only working it but wearing it on their sleeve (literally!) They are doing it not because they're forced to, but because they *want* to. It's about choice. They're choosing to do it.

Ask a youthpreneur what he or she hates most. The answer: bullshit. Don't try to give us a snow job. We want eveything real. Real information. Real guidance. Real substance. And we can spot the fakes. And because we demand real, we get real. We challenge authority more, we question the status quo. But we're not all business. You want us to work? Then bring the fun and the non conventional attitudes, even the quirkiness. We created the anti-suit culture. Yes—T-shirts in the board room...if we even have one. No corner office; we'll take the garage. All these corporate institutions talk about "fun" but very few actually live it. It's become relegated to another corporate tagline but it doesn't have be. I do one-to-one meetings over a game of ping pong or pool. It's for fun but it's not ONLY for fun. Doing this makes your company memorable, and if a guest has a good time they're more likely to refer customers to you and increase your bottom line. There's practical sense behind just having a great time. And we're proving it each and every day, as we reinvent how we start, grow and run our businesses.

Chapter I

What's Your Game Plan?

*"Do Not Seek to Follow in the Footsteps of the Men of Old;
Seek What they Sought."*

—*Basho*

Know Your Industry (Absolutely Nothing Stupid About
That)

First and foremost, you must intimately know the
industry you plan to enter. Ideally, it's always best to work
for someone else in that industry to learn the ins and outs
of it before going out on your own. However, if you are a
youthpreneur, you need to glean that knowledge from other
sources. So, how can you do that? Well, just do what I did.
I read literally a hundered stories about the junk hauling
business. I went to page 15 of Google, and no one goes
that deep – we read anything we could get our hands on
to get some kind of insight into how others in this business
actually operate.

What kind of things did we find? The detail was pretty amazing. We discovered how many jobs these companies were doing in a day, how the seasonality affects the business, how they market themselves, what their target market is—as well as what makes an ideal customer, what a day in the life looks like, "horror stories," mistakes other people made that we could learn from. (Let someone else be stupid.)

Then we learned a few things in a "trial by fire" fashion—not our favorite method; it hurts, but it works. There were the regulatory issues—this is the easy one to forget. We temporarily found ourselves out of busines because of it. You see, the State Department of Environmental Protection sent us a little "love letter". Believe it or not, you can't just dump your junk any where you want. What a concept! Who'd a thunk it? Just so you know, that "oops" set us back a year and a half. Expectations and reality don't always match.

Jeff's Stupid Mistake (Yes, I learned from it)

Here's another early stage blunder. First a guy called in and said he had a tank of some sort…typically when I heard tank I thought of a water heater tank; so I thought no problem, that's easy. I failed to ask what KIND of a tank – big mistake! When I get there it's not some 50 gallon water heater, it's a 500 gallon OIL tank and that is a big one. At the time, I couldn't get help from one of my friends (and I had no employees at the time), so I basically had to push it up into the truck myself with a little help from the customer. Thankfully he was at least a reasonably strong guy. Since I had already agreed on the price (without seeing it! Another early lesson) I couldn't increase it at this point without hurting our company name, so I just focused on hauling it away. Miraculously, we got it onto the truck without any macherinery (but maybe a few back aches!)

When I went to drop it off at the scrap yard they told me "No can do"—because even though 490 gallons of the oil were drained there was still 10 gallons left and oil tanks are extremely carefully regulated. So I asked, "How on earth was I supposed to get rid of it?" Then the scrapyard guy said, "No problem; just cut the thing in half and drain the oil yourself." Cut it in half! You've got to be kidding. I don't have the ability to do that. However, I didn't have any other option so I went out to buy a metal grinder so that I could at least cut a big hole in it. Only problem was that it was a massive tank that I just barely managed to get into our truck so I had to saw the thing open while it was still in the closed box truck. There were sparks flying everywhere including directly into the oil, which was kind of terrifying. Finally, once it was open I filled it with cat litter to soak up the remaining oil and then scooped the saturated cat litter out. NO PROBLEM, I thought. (Count on it.) I then brought it back to the scrap metal place to get rid of it. When I went back they still said it wasn't good enough. Not Good enough???? What a nightmare.

At this point I was totally defeated, but luckily my father had the smart idea to go to a gas station since they deal with oil all the time. The gas station owner helped me siphon out the oil without any issue. However, as I was leaving the gas station, the owner mentioned to me, "Hey, it's too bad you put a hole in that tank because I could have bought it off you and used it throughout the winter." AWESOME! Glad I know that now. Well at least when I went back to the scrap yard for the third time they finally accepted it and my (soggy) oil tank saga was over.

Howdy, Partner...

So, there's an up side and a down side to having company along for the ride—you know, partners. Partners can share the work load, share the investment and other risks and can often complement your weakest skills with their strongest ones. That's the up side. But, as we all know, what comes up can also come down. It's great when it works, but it's torture when it doesn't. It can even turn into an ugly "divorce." By all means give it a fair chance. But, at the same time, ya gotta admit when it just isn't working out. You know, that conversation you have with yourself in the bathroom—the "What was I thinking?" one. How do you avoid making it more painful than it has to be when it's time to go 'splitsville'? By setting things up right from the start. If you're going to have partner(s), spell everything out right from day number one. Put it in writing. Chisel it in stone. Paint a mural. Have everyone sign off on it. 'Nuff said. So, let's dig a little deeper into the dirt on this one.

When I started the company it was actually with a partner. The one thing that I got from it was the confidence to set out and start the company by reducing the risk and by the division of labor. There were other benefits. I thought – okay, this guy isn't going to want to screw this up either – we're in this together—hey, we can help each other not fail. (Now, that's a real show of confidence.) Another important benefit—we each had different skill sets. I was more of the marketing/branding/sales guy and he was more the operations/finance guy. Bringing two skill sets to the table can be huge. It's key to make sure though that your partner is strong in your weak areas and vice versa. It doesn't do much good to have two people good at the same things as you both reinforce the weak areas.

So, who owns how much of what? The first major issue is the equity split. When I started we did what most people think would be logical—50/50 partners. The thought was that we both were in this together and we're both contributing equally, so why wouldn't we both have equal equity? WRONG!!!!!!!!!!!!!!!!!!!!! This could not be more wrong. It needs to be at the minimum a 51/49 split. Otherwise there is no tie-breaker. You can easily get stuck in stalemates and deadlocked, which hurts productivity, morale and decision making speed—all of which can paralyze a young company...as it did with us.

So, how do you decide who gets the 51 percent? Well, first keep in mind that the 51 percent is more symbolic—it doesn't mean more money or more importance or even more authority. You both engage together on all the decisions. It still means that you have to hash it out when you have a disagreement. The 51 percent guy doesn't all of a sudden get to steamroll all the choices. It simply means that if you get into a deadlock situation, then you can default to the 51 percent guy for the ultimate decision. And this is also key, because by having that in place you avoid the resentment. Resentment can form if the tie-break just goes to the most aggressive person. While there is no easy way of deciding who gets the 51 percent, I would say it's the person who either thought of the idea first, or has made any kind of legitimate and significant investment or contribution. No real differences? Hey, you can always flip a coin. It's still worth it in that case to prevent a deadlock.

If that's a little too haphazard for you then you can always bring in a 3rd party impartial mediator. A mediator is a great way to solve things more objectively and democratically without resorting to litigation. Less costly and less contentious. Typically, in any divorce (business or personal), It costs 1/7th the amount to get a mediator compared to going to court.

Push aside the ego. By nature entrepreneurs more frequently have larger egos because it comes with the territory. You need to have the confidence and belief in yourself to start the company, so chances are you're not going to think you are some worthless plebian. AND they're highly emotionally invested in their business because they are founders. Someone who works at a corporate job has a lot less emotional investment.

Unstupid Partnerships

LET ME SAY THIS VERY **LOUDLY**. Make sure your paperwork (agreement) is rock solid from the beginning.

Do your best to determine in advance how compatible the partners are. How? Here are a few suggestions: Have each partner independently write out what his or her vision is for the company, what your company's and your personal exit strategy is, how many hours you're each willing to put in, what you want the culture of the business to be like, etc, etc. If you see that there are some serious discrepancies, you have to address them early on and see if it's still a good idea to become partners. Get a preview of what the dispute will be like BEFORE starting and not when you're waist deep in it, because it will only get more intense. It's easier to have a small disappointment at the start then a massive disappointment later on.

DIVISION OF LABOR is not a government agency. It's a decision you need to make before you start the business. Just exactly who will perform what functions. You and your partners can't have the same job title and responsibilities. One of the biggest mistakes I made with my partner earlier on was that we both had the same job title (stupid). We both did sales, operations, finance, marketing, the jobs, technology, etc, etc. As a result, we were always comparing each other's work to the other person's. For example, if we're both responsible for sales but one person is stronger in sales, then we start thinking that they are not doing their job, when in reality their time would be better spent doing what they do best.

So, how do you share the wealth when the business starts making money—just divide it into equal parts? Guess again. Make it an educated guess. When it comes to compensation, different work should command different pay scales, based on its value to the enterprise. You need to come up with a formula to make sure it's based on *performance*. Establish how you get paid for what you do. If you do different work then you get paid accordingly. This avoids having one person getting paid based on the other person's work. It needs to be established before the work really gets started so you can sign off on it when you're both being objective and avoid disputes later on.

You must have an operating agreement signed by all partners on day 1 of the business. It is absolutely essential to have an operating agreement for not only compensation but for all areas of the business. You can call it your business pre-nup! That includes your financial contribution, your roles and job titles, hours to be working on the business, how disputes will be settled and most importantly—what to do when someone's plan changes. Maybe at some point someone is working more or less or wants to get out of the business, or simply wants to change his or her role. The agreement also regulates the partners' interests in any outside interests that might be competing with the business, responsibility for record keeping and what happens with a death or the dissolution of the business. This needs to be spelled out with clear heads beforehand. It is MOST important to do with friends (and family), the people you think you don't need to do this with. A lot of assumptions can be made and later on if there is a conflict, because those assumptions were never clarified, now all of a sudden everything becomes personal. While I was lucky to retain as a friend my previous business partner, I know numerous people who have lost friends and even family members over partnership disputes. The worst part is that because our memories of the past can be fallible it's easy to misconstrue events and simply not be objective. It's best to have this drafted by a qualified business attorney before the commencement of the business and signed by all partners. There's a saying in Spanish, "When all is clear, we preserve the friendship."

Like any other business contract, if it's submitted to a judge, ultimately the outcome will depend upon the "intent of the parties"—whether it's to haul junk or start a business together. So if you clarify the intent up front there is less opportunity for discrepancies, misconstruing and lack of clarity. You take away the gray areas of "Oh, that's what I meant and that's what you meant." This is done to protect the company. You have to think of the company as a separate entity from yourself. Think of it as your child and your partner as your spouse. How would you want your child treated? Both you and your partners have the same interest in that child's welfare.

"Find People Smarter Than You. It Proves How Smart You Are." (Nothing Stupid About That)

Know Your Strengths. Nobody excels at everything. Do the "mirror, mirror on the wall" thing if you have to. Take an inventory of your skills. Then rank them from best to worst. Would you hire you to do the things at the bottom of the list? This is 'get real' time. The best advice anyone ever gave me? Find people smarter than you. It just makes sense. (And it proves how smart you are.) Then there's that other thing I can't help myself from doing. I'm always picking other people's brains— I would

say border line harassing them for information. I learned a
secret about myself: I don't have all the answers. The good news
is that you don't need all the answers, but you do need to be able
to ask great questions. I found that thoughts normally crystalize
best while talking with other people, rather than mulling them
over in my head constantly. How far have I gone with this?
Did I ever approach someone totally random—like at a urinal
or a walk-in freezer or something and ask for their opinion?

Or an unusual person. Like the owner of 1-800-Got Junk (my
competitor). Answer: YES. I admit it. I got an introduction
and he was nice enough to chat with me. Who knows? That
competitor could acquire us one day. Ya never know.

Strength in Numbers

Drum roll...this is a biggie. Know when to delegate. It could
not only mean the life or death of your business; it could
mean your own life or death. Too many people have over
worked themselves in the name of heroic entrepreneurship.
I found myself hiring haulers to help me with my junk
removal business after just 9 months – pretty much the
second I could afford to do so. Before that, I was sending
emails as late as 11PM at night, I was hauling from 6AM to
7PM and then squeezing in some networking meetings and
returning phone calls any 2 seconds I was not lifting a couch
myself. I found myself driving the truck, steering wheel in
one hand and sandwhich in the other, with my cell phone
on the shoulder. Worse yet, here I was, carrying a couch,
the phone rings – I give one look to my co-lifter and he just
looks and he's like "No, you don't get that call," but I had to
get it. Not taking care of yourself? Definitely stupid.

"Spend Your Time on The Stuff That Brings in the Money"

Probably just as important as knowing when it's time to hire help is knowing when to outsource. Like we said, you can't be great at everything. Besides, you gotta spend your time on the stuff that brings in the money. With that thought

firmly burned into my brain, I got a bookkeeper after just 4 months. So, here was one of my blunders before I made that decision.

If Money Doesn't Grow on Trees, so Where Does it Grow?

I met with my accountant and asked her, "Cash goes into my personal account and checks go into my business account, right?" She replied, "No; you can't put ANY money into your account. That's the point of 'under the table.' "So, I was like, "Ah, what do you do, put it in a shoebox under your bed?" She responded with, "Uhh, yeah, basically—but I really don't advise doing that either." So, I learned the BIG lesson: the value of doing everything the right way—by the books and ON the books. I make a big deal of reporting all of my income because it makes my books look better—which means better potential for business loans and lines of credit that will actually allow my business to grow and thrive.

The Health-Wealth Connection

We consulted psychologist, author and professor Diane Lang on how to handle the intense amount of stress that comes crashing down on startup and early stage entrepreneurs. So, how do we avoid burnout, doc? Diane explains that, in an effort to try to handle everything, we struggle to achieve life-work balance, putting ourselves at the bottom of the priority list. How can we perform effectively and efficiently if we don't take care of ourselves? Here are our (very smart) psychologist's recommendations (couch not required—but could be useful).

Diane recommends we start by keeping a "Journal of Truth" to answer the question – are your basic needs met? She recommends we track these critical items:

- Sleep
- What you are eating and when – not going for long periods of time without eating
- Water
- Did you exercise today?
- For one week, keep a journal and write down your sleep, exercise, what you eat and the water you drink. Do not make any changes— just review what was done and see what's causing you to feel off balance physically.

Diane relates that we deny stress, and as we become preoccupied we forget—but our bodies are fully aware and eventually display physical, emotional and psychosomatic signs. What to do?

To prevent burn out, Diane recommends we engage in a "Daily Dump" (No, not that kind.) right before bed. Here's what you do.

At night, when you are quiet and not in panic mode, write out all of what you need to get done the next day. By getting it out and off your mind, it helps you sleep, rather than worrying about what you "should have done." Then either hand write or enter in your computer all of what you need to do the next day. This helps us sleep. As our expert reminds us, without 7-8 hours of sleep, we experience big consequences. After the third night of six hours or fewer of sleep, cognition falls off (and it's tough to put it back on).

Diane reminds us of the importance of daily exercise. At LEAST walk; it creates mindfulness – peace and solitude. If you do this four times a week for 20-30 minutes, it's fine. Walking produces endorphins, the happy chemical, while reducing the stress hormone cortisol – thereby naturally de-stressing you.

Wait, there's more! Part of the day, just UNPLUG – do nothing with technology. Dinner time is a good one for this. You need the down time and a specific time at night that you are off of everything tech related, in order to refresh and refuel yourself. Diane further recommends you stay off of technology before you go to bed. You won't sleep well if you are plugged in before bed time.

To really achieve as much of a balanced cycle as you can, make sure to book 1-2 vacations a year—even if it's just long weekends or a daycation where you go local. It's important to celebrate holidays, birthdays, etc—especially as an entrepreneur. Even if you can't take a full week since you work for yourself. Most important: create some hard stops – limitations—have a social life. The number one factor to happiness is socialization. Delegate parts of your work to other people; those functions you don't like or are not good at. You can always be part time if you can't afford to get started; use a VA (virtual assistant). Ultimately, it costs more money to do stuff that takes you forever. And folks, our psychologist knows best. Diane says, NO MORE MULTITASKING— it adds stress to our life. When we do it, we never give anything 100% and we wind up having to do the project over again because it's sub par. (Author's note: Isn't that stupid?) We need to give our work full attention and full creativity.

So, is there any hope for the workaholic, those who are hopelessly addicted to work? What can you do if you just can't stop? Sadly, Diane confirms that we can only help people who want to make the change. Some people have to hit their own rock bottom. Usually it's their health that suffers or they have a panic attack. A good social life, good health and sleep is GOOD FOR THE BOTTOM LINE. It starts with awareness – that's why we need the journal.

Young people are the biggest violators; they think nothing can happen to them. Some think they can live without sleep because they don't feel the effects as quickly, but the burnout will come. Diane observes that Millenials don't want to work as hard; they are more about purpose and meaning.

See Diane Lang's website: www. dlcounseling.com

Chapter II

Picking Your Idea/Forecasting Business Trends

"Talent Hits a Target No One Else Can Hit. Genius Hits a Target No On Else Can See."

—*Arthur Schopenhauer*

How can you succeed if you're in the wrong business to begin with? Figure out what you can expect to become and to remain popular five years from now—not by doing what appears solid now. Don't just be looking myopically right now—look for what's coming down the pike. If it's already BIG, then it's too late for you to get in. Why be an "also ran?" You have to identify emerging markets and future trends—to understand where things are going. Identify and anticipate growth areas in business. How can we identify them?

If you hear the phrase, "Oh, it's way too early for that," it's probably a good indicator of where you want to be looking. Take for example, electric cars. A lot of people really resist change because we've had 100 years of the internal combustion engine tradition. (Dirty little secret: electric cars came first! And they were much cleaner.) The world is littered with examples of both companies and people who were slow to adapt. For example, the makers of Blackberry (mistakenly) believed people NEED a tactile keyboard. While it was true at the time, there was still a market segment that embraced this, it was quickly eroding! You have to look at the trends. Take the publishing business. This book was published by print-on-demand technology. The major publishing companies didn't think it would ever take off and buried their heads in the sand (because they were afraid of the prediction), but those same companies are now buying stakes in the new publishing technologies.

There has been no greater innovator in the past twenty or so years than Apple®, introducing the iPod, the iPad and the iPhone. No one thought they needed these things. I even read a book by a prominent branding expert who said that the camera phone would never take off because no one would want one mediocre product to perform multiple functions instead of two highly effective ones. Well, look how that turned out! (Even experts can say stupid things.)

Follow the Money

Here's another place to watch for emerging trends: look at angel and VC funding awards; see who is getting the money. These folks do their due diligence and are typically always looking for the ideas that are ahead of the curve – the ones that are bubbling up in that small community before they become a major well known idea across the world. Similary, look for business incubators and accelerators – they harbor companies that usually do not have major funding yet, but could show promise and could very well take off down the line.

Fad vs Trend

So, how do you know the difference between a fad and a trend? First, look to see who is associated with the idea, product or service. If something gets a big celebrity endorsement it could just be a popularity bubble. Look at how much potential the item has for line extension. If it looks like something that can be extended, it probably has legs—but if it looks like a one-off it can probably get eclipsed by some newer, better technology. Take, for example, QR codes! Everyone (even older people) thought that it was the way of the future—so, why did it fizzle? They were supposed to make it easy to scan instead of type in a website address. While it was a cool idea in theory, it requires a mass adoption of everyone to get on board, but the benefit wasn't that important or helpful. Then there was Google Glass? Maybe this will be big some day, but at the writing of this book there was a lot of hype about it and not much actually happening. Why? Because it has to be something that's really filling a need or making things super convenient without much hassle. But if you have to go through a lot of effort for something that is supposed to save effort, then it kind of defeats the purpose. Maybe future iterations will prove to be successful, but at the time, it's simply not the case.

The product or service idea doesn't have to be a high tech trend; it can be a basic market trend. I selected my industry because with the baby boomers and the staggering number of retirees downsizing their residences, and people having smaller families, there is a ton of clutter reduction that will follow. Any business related to elder care is a good one. In-home healthcare companies are exploding in growth, for example.

Look at how technology is going to impact the field or area or product scope. Personally, I really love a good notebook. For a brief time I considered doing some kind of print products. While people are still printing things all the time today, the trend is consistently shrinking and there's no logical reason to think that would stop. It doesn't make sense to invest in a shrinking market.

On occasion, trends can be reversed to an extent. For example, with a lot of digital websites there was a push for more global connection and exposure. Take for example, Facebook®. As that platform began exploding, at the same time people felt the impersonality. So, in a way things began to also get hyper local in various online niches.

"Find an Unserved or Underserved Niche" (Way Beyond Stupid!)

Let's adress the "passion" question. People are constantly tossing around the word passion when it comes to business. You should pick something that you're madly passionate about. For example, if you love cycling then you need to start some kind of cycling company or a product or service that can be used by cycling companies. However, I find that the reality is that first and foremost your goal is to find something that you can do better than the current offerings. Find something that fills a NEED in the marketplace—a gap—An UNSERVED or UNDERSERVED niche. When you're running your cycling based product, your goal everyday is to grow a business—you are a business person, not a cycling person. Two very different things. What you need to be excited about is developing the business, growing customers, staking your claim in the market place-and that has nothing to do with cycling. Ultimately, the growth areas are ones that require specialized skills.

Jeff's Big Hint: To really get a handle on the growing trends, watch the next generation. Study their behaviors, their priorities and their mindset. That will give you a clue as to what the trend will be – notice their different interests and concerns. At this writing, it's the Millennials. They exhibit different career preferences – they're not as money motivated, they value flexibility in work schedules as a high priority and they place more emphasis on fun than previous generations. That gives a you clue as to what business would appeal to them as consumers. Since they are the up and coming generation that will grow in spending power, you want to grow with them. They are your future customers. It's not even too early to look at generation Z because even though at the moment it's premature, the goal is to think 10 years down the line. Even though now they don't have the spending power, they will soon have influence on the principal of the household as they hit a certain age – more of a say in what the family is spending on.

Chapter III

Understanding Finances

"It is Vain to do More With What Can be Done With Less"

—*William Occam*

What Comes in Must Go Out

Bills, bills, bills. So much for that "pay yourself first stuff." If you want to stay in business, you have to pay your help, pay your suppliers and yes, pay the tax man...and pay them on time. It's kind of like what mom and dad used to try and tell you about how they ran the household. No Christmas bonus? Sorry, no vacation this year. Ya gotta know your numbers—what it costs to put the key in the door every day before you take in a dime from a customer... and before you take out a dime for yourself. It's a lot easier to do that today with the inexpensive, easy computerized accounting tools. You can start pulling reports from the system as soon as you have a few months of history in your business. Then you have some bench marks to start making projections and "what if" scenarios from. Hey, this stuff really works!

"Hold Off As Long As Possible Before Taking Any Outside Capital...Until You Have Leverage"

So, let's talk about your financing. Before you ever open your doors, you should have a pretty good idea of what it will cost you to start and run your business. Of course, there's always the unforeseen. But, we'll deal with that later. So, hopefully you've been smart enough to either stay in mom and dad's basement as long as you can or maybe in the tree house they built you in the backyard when you were a kid. Where am I going with this? Yes, you need to have saved up some of your own money to invest in your businesss. (I know, in the internet age they don't have paper routes. They do still wash cars and mow lawns, don't they?) Anyway, we call it your skin in the game. Wise investors always say, if you're not putting *your* money in, why should I put any of mine in? Here's my most sage advice. Are you ready? Hold off as long as possible before taking any outside capital. Why? Because at the start you have no leverage, so you're guaranteed to be screwed unless that's the only option. But I would even challenge that notion – get a bunch of micro loans from credit cards and family. (Ya know, beg, borrow, but don't steal.) What did he mean by "get screwed?" Well, you will either pay through the nose with a high interest loan, sap your business's cash flow while paying back the loan—or worse yet, lose control (and your share of ownership) to the people putting in the money. Did you think they were really that nice? (That would be stupid.)

You need to learn about The Cost of Money. Not surprisingly, there's cheap money and then there's expensive money. Credit cards are the expensive money. Try to get zero interest credit cards, as long as you have a plan to pay them off quickly. And family is cheap money and enhances your cash flow. Try to support yourself off of cash flow as much as possible. I got one credit card with zero percent interest for 18 months. Protect your credit score as religiously as if you were a priest, a nun, a monk, a rabbi or an imam. Refinance your balance later at a lower interest rate when the business is established. Remember, your payment track record is your golden key (smart).

No matter what, you must budget for taxes—and workers comp and insurance. Know thy numbers. Data data, data. Payroll taxes? Go by the book. Shortcuts will make you short on results. Create a separate account just for taxes. Don't let yourself think that you actually have that money.

Devaluing Money—Trial by Fire: Jeff's Second Stupid Mistake

We all have at least one big blunder story to tell from our early days in business. Here was ours. Let's just call it "The concrete job." It went like this. We took away concrete that cost us $350 in disposal charges, $30 in travel expenses, $70 in labor costs and we quoted the job for $400. and ended up doing it for $200. Any fool can tell that's a losing deal, so what happened? Looks are deceiving. It appeared to be just a small pile of stuff. We charge by volume and volume-wise it was not a ton of stuff. However, because the stuff was so heavy it cost us an exorbitant amount to dump it. Evidently, we didn't look closely enough.

Obviously, there was a flaw in our pricing formula. The moral of the story: you gotta check and double check all of your costs before you quote charges to your customer.

Bootstrapping vs. OPM (Other People's Money—yes, they made a movie by that title. Look it up!) When we started our company, we figured we would do the guerilla marketing thing, so we put up paper flyers. Ya know, cheap advertising. Well, we almost got a summons because people thought we were trying to rob them since we were trying to be savvy marketers and target our clientele by posting in the wealthier neighborhoods. Being the aspiring big time operation we were, we eventually moved on to lawn signs, which were clearly more legitimate and professional looking (why not, politicians get away with it? So do realtors, for the record). They are inexpensive but they don't devalue your brand; many people see them so they do get a lot of big-time exposure.

Ya gotta be thrifty when you're not cash-rich. We bought a used truck from U-Haul when we started out. A new dump truck would have cost us upwards of $65,000. U-Haul had one listed for $8,000. and we negotiated it down to $5,000. (pretty smart, eh?) When that's all you can afford, it makes you think about and handle money smarter. And that truck is STILL in use today. Even though now we can afford brand new dump trucks, we're still using our good old original one and not over-extending ourselves. The first three of our hauling trucks were also bought used. We had to make a few compromises, but they saved us a lot of money when we needed them. For the cost of a new paint job, most of them looked as good as new! At the same time, ya gotta know the difference between frugality and foolishness. You can "be on a shoestring but not on a tightrope". Our very first vehicle was a 1992 Dodge van. We bought it for only $600. It was quite a piece of work. It was technically a white van but you would never know that. There were all sorts of special colors forming on the outside. Mechanically, it wasn't much better. In order to drive straight, you'd have to drive with your hands all the way to the left. Every once in a while it would even billow smoke into the cab. That was not fun. We affectionately nicknamed it "the rolling death trap." (Definitely stupid.) Thankfully, it never officially lived up to it's name because we're all still here. Not a good plan if you want to keep your team. Know when "to spend or not to spend." (Apologies to Shakespeare.)

Then there was the matter of office space. We started out with the third floor attic of a converted house. We got a great deal on it and it did the trick (a little toasty during the summer). As much as I would love fancy digs, they were unnecessary and it would be silly to try and justify them. The walk-up was tough, but once I was no longer working the trucks myself, I needed the exercise anyway!

We had to get creative when it came to parking the trucks, too. At startup, we found friends who owned businesses in the area and parked them at their places. They weren't hidden in some industrial park, but were out in the roadway getting (signage) exposure and actually bringing in more money. Pretty smart, eh? Sometimes doing it on the cheap can yield even better outcomes. And, we didn't even have to pay for a billboard!

"Sometimes you have to GO SMALL to GET BIG." When scaling your business it's a constant rollercoaster ride of cash, and therefore your emotions. This is particularly true if you are in a seasonal business. In our company, we make over half of our year's profit in just 3 months. This can make dealing with cash flow quite a challenge. Some companies have it even worse. Toys R Us® makes nearly all of their profit in a measly 5 weeks during the holiday season. If they have one Saturday that gets hit by a bad snow storm, that could mean the difference between a profitable year and an unprofitable one. As a result, you need to be extremely careful when planning out your cash flow.

It is key to know when to spend and when not to spend. You have to get the timing just right. Think about trigger events that affect your business. As I mentioned, in the early days of our company, we had a small office and a small warehouse that were in different locations which created a whole host of problems. We were dying to get a new combined space. I was very tempted to pull the trigger because I had the money in my account. However, it was at the end of our busy season, and after doing some basic forecasting I realized that even if we somehow pulled it off, it would be a noose around our neck. All we'd be focused on and thinking about and working towards would be making our monthly nut instead of focusing on our key long term goals. It's good to be bold when scaling but you have to know when to go small to (eventually) get big. When we chose to hold off until just before the next busy season, we shored up our cash reserves, got ourselves into a very healthy financial positon and then pulled the trigger when the timing was right.

The ideal time to make significant investments in growth is usually just before you need to. If you jump on it too soon you can put yourself out of business, and if you jump on something too late you can stall your business. Making the investment should scare you a little bit – that way you know that you're focusing on growth—but not terrify you so that your business becomes paralyzed. If you're not a little scared then you're playing it too safe. But if you're not sleeping, then you're playing it too loose.

Now we have a great, spacious warehouse, but it wasn't always that way. In the VERY beginning, when we didn't have too many jobs to do, my parents were nice enough to let me use one bay in their garage as temporary storage for stuff we couldn't immediately dispose of, or that we needed to do bulk runs to a donation location. Pretty cool, since they weren't charging me rent. However, eventually their garage was turning into a junkyard. We still didn't want to spend money on a warehouse, so we rented a large storage unit. That did the trick for the rest of our first year. Soon after, even though we weren't actively looking for a warehouse, our office landlord had some spare warehouse space in the back of his building. That became our next (cost conscious) stepping stone. It wasn't perfect but it met our immediate needs and it allowed us to save enough money to eventually move into the great warehouse we have now.

Chapter IV

What's Your Style

"A Mediocre Person Tells. A Good Person Explains. A Superior Person Demonstrates. A Great Person Inspires Others to See for Themselves."

—*Harvey Mackay*

If you're going to own and operate a business—any business, you gotta have people skills. You can't just be a great technician or a great craftsman. If you're not willing to work on your people skills, then just get a job. People are everything. A business is only as good as the people in it and their ability to work with other people—and that includes staff, clients and vendors. So, let's take the solopreneur. When it's all you and you are the company, how you relate to people and interact is pretty much everything for how people view and think about the business. To them, you *are* the business. Beyond that, without good people skills, you won't attract people to you—valuable vendors, talented employees and especially those tasty customers. Mirror time again! So, ask yourself, would I want to do business with me?

Your Management Style

If you got far enough in business to get people to work for you, don't assume they are here to stay forever. Today, the average person changes jobs about every three years. That said, ask yourself what makes people want to STAY with you? The traditional "Command and Control" management style doesn't work any more. The older generation that grew up on this model says to just tell employees to do it because "you're the boss! That's it." "Well, then your employees will most likely reply, "Fine, we'll do what you say but we're going to pull out our job description and only do the bare minimum and all that extra shit you want us to do, going above and beyond, staying late and showing up early and taking extra time with customers, and coming in on short notice, etc, etc. is not going to happen any more." At that point, your employees are just going to look out for themselves. (Now, that would be stupid, wouldn't it?)

At one point, we were trying to implement new marketing initiatives by having our employees market the company. We had an issue with people actually doing the promotional tasks we wanted them to do. My initial reaction was to bring the hammer down and reprimand them for not doing it and issue punishments. I tried that and, MAJOR FAIL. Enforcement is a reaction to the problem, but it didn't fix the underlying problem. Going about it with this approach just pushed my employees further away. When I changed that and instead had a conversation about why it wasn't getting done and tried to understand what was going on, I realized that it was mostly just a training issue! They weren't clear enough on why it needed to be done and didn't even really understand how everything worked. I just assumed that because I understand how to promote the company that they would automatically know how to do it. Also, the task must be incentivized properly if all of a sudden you want people to be doing extra work above and beyond their job description. Once I understood where they were coming from better, I was able to address concerns and build the training in that they needed. Then the issue dramaticly improved.

"Allow Them to Make Mistakes and Correct Their Own Mistakes"

In this millenium, I suggest instead that you get the guys' (or gals') input. In our business, I often ask my employees things such as how they would approach a certain job, or what extra tools and supplies would best set them up for getting the job done successfully—or even what people on our staff would be the best suited to work on a particular project. In short, the newer paradigm is a participatory mangement style. Ask your staff for their opinions about how you should do things because they're doing the actual work all day. Hey, that's the best focus group you can get! Use their intel on the ground. It's gonna benefit you and your company. Take it a step further. Give them a say in managing themselves and their work load. Give them some more discretion and allow them to make mistakes and to correct their own mistakes.

Treat them like kids? Not unless you want to go back to working alone. When it comes to the "D" word—Discipline, instead of issuing harsh punishments or Draconian penalities, ask them what they would like to do to 'make things right'. For example, in our business, one guy did the math wrong during billing and lost us $200 bucks. I could say, "Hey, pay that back now; you owe it or you're gonna be punished", but it was an honest mistake and it's more important to just learn from it. I asked him what he would like to do to make things right and he offered to take a day to market our business for free and that resulted in a new job that brought in $600. Hmmm, maybe we should make more mistakes!! In addition to formal perfomance reviews, give on-the-spot feedback quickly – both victories and mistakes, so that they can learn quickly and adjust quickly. At the same time, make sure there are some kind of consequences for not following procedures. On the other side of the coin, sometimes an owner will try to avoid conflict and push things under the rug, but that leads to an undisciplined business, which is equally undesirable.

"Know When to Use the Hammer and When to Use Honey"

While we are spending a lot of time discussing a participatory employee style of management, at the same time you have to differentiate between something that should be a collaborative conversation, and at other times you have to know when rules, in order to have a structured well functioning company, simply have to be enforced. For example, if it is our policy to wear a uniform but people are not wearing the uniform, then you MUST enforce it— otherwise people will not take your policies seriously and everything you say will become optional. You don't want to be a jerk about things but the consequence of letting people walk all over you can stagnate and cause your company to fail. The key is being able to know the difference between these two scenarios. Know when to use the hammer and when to use honey.

Don't forget to reward your people. Celebrate milestones and victories. Go out for drinks and share the wealth. Go out as a team. We instituted a bonus system. If the guys do excellent and profits are really high, we give them some of that back as a bonus to incentivize them further.

Let's not forget the other "D" word—delegation. Unless you are a superhero, you're gonna have to learn how to do this. Here's how the scary new experience went for me. It was about 6 months into our business and I was doing so many jobs; I was at a job myself and it was running late. I had an interview to go to hire for a hauler position, but we had just gotten to the job and I both desperately needed to finish the job and to hire the hauler to avoid this exact situation. Luckily the guy I was working with had a friend in the area who he called and asked to jump in. He said, "Hey, it's okay; go to your inteview and I'll get the job done." I had a million questions for him: Do you know what to bill? What are you going to do if he has any objections? Do you know any of the parking issues? Just general freaking out, HOLDING BACK, afraid to delegate (acting just a little bit stupid). And then I finally said 'screw it', I'll let you do it and pray. There's no right best only thing to do. I had to get past the fear and trust that he would get the job done for me. So then I was able to go do the interview; it went well, I was able to hire the guy shortly after and my worker came back with the check. Of course, I asked him a million questions again, but everything was totally fine, so the lesson learned was you gotta let go and trust other people to get stuff done. Trust their training. (Or train them better!)

Here's how smart delegation can work for you: ENROLL THE EMPLOYEES IN THE SOLUTION: It's the difference between giving orders and people taking OWNERSHIP of their own plan. Present the goal and make it clear WHERE we need to get to and WHY, so they understand the purpose behind it. Then get them to help figure out HOW to get there. Say, we are HERE now folks, how do we get THERE? Now it's THEIR PLAN, not mine, and they're gonna wanna make sure that THEIR plan is successful.

THE 4 STEP PROCESS TO DELEGATION:

THE KEY TO DELEGATION IS MAKE IT A REQUEST, NOT A DEMAND. The way to do it is to start with *this is why* I need to delegate, therefore I needed to get this off my plate. Then say, "This is why I think you're a good choice." Then ask, "Are you willing to take that on?" If they say no, then ask, "What do I need to take care of so you can take this on?" If they say just handle A and then I can do it, then respond, "Okay, if A is done, THEN can you do it?" If they still say no, ask "What ELSE do you need to take this on?" First enroll them to take it on; then you can talk details and they will ask questions about it.

If managers communicate clear instructions, there should be minimal need for discipline—unless, of course, employees simply don't follow them. Furthermore, if you let people know what you want them to do, they will come up with a solution... so you don't have to, at every turn. The vast majority of world problems involve a breakdown of communication. People stop talking. People start speculating. People get rumors and misinformation that starts getting paraded around as truth. Now, all of a sudden no one works well together any more; people are at odds. You have a boat where people are rowing in different directions. You get the visual. It happens all the time and often times you may not even realize that it's happening.

When all is said and done, you have to confront difficult situations. Painful? Yes, but you need to avoid the "nice guy syndrome"—letting your need to be liked overwhelm your better judgment. Run your business with your head, but still have a heart. *Don't skip performance reviews*. While current thinking says they are going out the window in favor of more immediate, fast, on the spot feedback, without them how do you document poor performance? The NICE thing about them is that you get to say all the GOOD things they're doing too – so it's easier to make the good old "compliment sandwich". One way to make them more effective: have them do SELF REVIEWS. Ask your employees, "How do YOU think you're doing?" What areas do you think you're doing well in, and where do YOU think you need to improve? This will take some of the onus off of the owner, and it helps you to see if there are any mismatches in expectations that you simply did not realize. When your employees do self evaluation, let's suppose they say they are at a 6. A great question to ask: "What can I do to help you get to 10?" They're responsible for the outcome, but your offering help, support, assistance, insight and perspective—but the effort still comes from them. One thing to note: junior level people talk about behavior, while senior level people talk more about results.

Give POSITIVE REINFORCEMENT when things go well. It's easier to reinforce good behavior than to criticize bad behavior. CATCH PEOPLE DOING THINGS RIGHT. Psychological theory indicates that there are four ways to adress feedback – you can apply or withhold praise, or you can apply or withhold criticism. Normally we don't say anything— that's withholding praise. My best advice: don't say, "That was wrong," say, "This is what I would like to see," or "Let me show you how to do it." The majority of feedback should be positive reinforcement over negative reinforcment. Call people in to praise them for things *you're* trying to improve.

Get Creative with Incentives.

You can only get so far with money IF you're paying your people a reasonable amount and covering their basic needs. Think about what other things you can reward them with. PEOPLE ARE MOTIVATED BY DIFFERENT THINGS. Consider: time off, responsibility, work from home, etc. One of my employees came to me with what I thought to be devastating news—someone was willing to pay him significantly more than what I was paying him and also offered to pay his mortgage, as well as let him work from home. I told him, "No, we have to figure this out." I asked him, "What is really meaningful to you about the other company's job offer?" When we really got into it we realized that the extra pay was not actually a massive motivator; it was actually all about QUALITY OF LIFE. It was not having to stress about the mortgage and the flexibility of working from home when needed. We struck that deal and we both left happy. And I got to retain my key employee because of that conversation.

Sometimes it's the little things that count. People want to know their efforts are appreciated. That's the number one reason people leave a company. One of the best ideas a friend who owns a company talked to me about was THE PINK SLIP METHOD. We also affectionately refer to it as the "You Kicked Ass Award." It works like this: write what the employee <u>did right</u> and according to what CORE VALUE, and tell other people. Hand out the slips at the daily huddles. More than 10 pink slips a month and you get a $20 gift card to Starbucks® and the overall winner gets a $100 Dunkin Donuts gift card, or something similar. If you take care of your employees first, the product + service will follow.

We've talked a lot about how our generation sees business, work and life differently. For us, it's all about our values. "Always remember, alignment is not an event, it is a process." People need to be continually reminded of the company's core values. You need processes in place to create stories around the values. Even the owner can forget or make a decision not aligned with a key value—everyone needs value reinforcement. Here's another idea: at a meeting, have some of the team members nominate someone based on how well they lived your company values. If you instill those values, the employees will begin to self-police. (No badges needed.) We'll cover this aspect of running your business in more depth in the chapter on culture.

The Feedback Method

Yes, as the owner you're in charge. Still, it works best to ask the employee for permission. Use a method similar to the SBI Feedback Tool developed by The Center for Creative Leadership. "Can I give you some feedback?" (They have to be open to it.) They are responsible for the communication. If they say no, then ask, "Okay, when?" Focus on the THINGS – NOT the intent, NOT the feeling. *Only focus on the things that happened when you didn't do X.* It can't be disputable. It has to be indisputable facts. When X happened, this is the result. "Can you work on that?" Yes, you can do this *same* feedback loop for positive reinforcement as well! All feedback should be pretty immediate. Let's take a peek at an example of how this works.

FEEDBACK MODEL EXAMPLE

1. The Question... "Can I give you feedback?"
2. The Behavior... "When you're on your phone texting during the company meeting..."
3. The Result... "It distracts other people."
4. The Impact... "We don't get your feedback and would really love to hear what you have to say."

Most important, give feedback without judgment. Establish a Communcation Schedule:

- Hold a Daily Huddle
- Hold a weekly meeting for performance coaching and TRAINING

- Quarterly: review what the employees said they would improve and ask, "Where are you with that?" Look for a 70-80% increase in those areas.

Lack of communication leads to problems. Enforcing the policies needs to happen, but enforcement is a reaction to the problem; it doesn't correct the problem. The owner has to fix it when you have a lack of commitment to one another. You can never assume what morale is—you have to find out and then adjust your perception to the reality. It's your responsibility to get people to play nicely in the sandbox. (Give 'em a shovel, but don't let 'em bury one another.)

We said it before, but it bears repeating. Getting employees' buy-in to your mission is critical to your success. We are here ————→ we need to get there. Why? The reason we need to get to there is because we don't have the house we want, the car we want, the money we want, the benefits we want; so it's imperative now to talk about how we are going to do that. When it comes to procedures, step away. Have the *staff* prepare the checklists and then _they_ do audits on themselves. There's a check list and they meet to monitor themselves. This process builds trust – that you the owner trust them to do it. Put out a jar of honey. Pull them into the solution.

What to Do When It's Just Not Working...

I bring you this advice directly from a recent experience I had with a deteriorating employee relationship. When you approach the person, consider the following tactics:

1. Accusation vs. Observation: Don't accuse people, as there are a lot of possible reasons why something happened. Start by saying, "I've made a few observations." Put it from your point of view— "This is how I saw it." Treat it as a listening exercise. Ask, "What's your perspective on this?"

2. Focus on the Feelings: Tell them, "I've had some challenges with how we work together and it feels difficult for me. How does it feel for you? What's working and what isn't?" Come from an empathetic point of view. Explore both parties' feelings and needs. Go through the feelings you were having. *Ask them what they were feeling.*

3. Communication Breakdown: We had a conversation about X and I heard you say XYZ, so this is what I expected. Where did we break down in our communication? *Get the employee to open up and talk.*

4. "Non Violent Communication:"[1] "Assume positive intent." This person is not intending to be malicious. Something is going on and they think this is the best option they have.

5. There is a "Ladder of Inference[2]" at play here. Refer to observable facts in the stories you tell. Don't just fight on positions.

In this case, the ultimate outcome was to part ways so we don't have an acrimonious situation. If I didn't put it on the table, this would have dragged on forever.

---

[1] Marshall Rosenberg

[2] Chris Argyris

In the end, it all adds up to achieving the result. In order to do that, we need to manage <u>accountability.</u> How do we do that? Start with the task list – make sure it gets done. Every morning, pick 3-5 essential employee projects – the "must do's." Have THEM outline what they think those tasks should be (based on your larger objectives). Have a scorecard for each employee, with measurable metrics to track and monitor that they met their goals. Then establish new goals. Schedule a "Feedback Friday". Block out 3-5PM and schedule 15 minutes to talk with the owner about feedback. Ask each employee, "What do YOU think excellence looks like in a MEASURABLE WAY?" Get them INVESTED IN THE PROCESS. How do we come to an agreement on what excellence looks like? GET ON THE SAME PAGE. At first – there will be some pushback, but power through it. Put everyone's individual scorecard together to get a general consensus and share everyone's then at a team meeting. Have an open discussion about them. Figure out the connections. Look at your KPI's (Key Performance Indicators). Measure everything. How do we know that got done?

Learn From Others' Stupidity (It's Cheaper!)

Sometimes you have to turn the mirror around and do the opposite of what your former bosses did. I once worked for a micro-manager who would focus on minute things that were ultimately inconsequential, unproductive and based on outdated ideas. He did not look at the big picture and the results, so I was determined to be the exact opposite. The reverse holds true, too. Think about someone you worked for and really admired how they operated. Emulate them. I had good mentors that were totally customer centric about everything. They made decisions that went back to what's best for the customer.

"The Single Most Important Ability You Can Have: Think on Your Feet"

If you asked me what's the single most important trait you could have early in the life of your business, I would say it's the ability to think on your feet. Just think of all the things that can—and do, go wrong. Decisions have to be made and made quickly. Decisions that will affect your operation, your customer perceptions and even your staff's morale. Take for example, something as mundane as scheduling –when a job becomes twice the size of what you expected it to be, when a customer gives you inacurate details, when someone gets a flat tire; or, what happens when you have 10 jobs back to back and everything gets out of whack and the day the truck breaks down it's 100 degrees and pouring rain. Yeah, mom did say there would be days like this. This is what we signed up for. So, when it comes to your management style, ask yourself: are you a dictator, a priest, a referee or a diplomat?

One of the prime rules of effective leadership is always walking the walk. A lot of times people want to lead by ordering people to do things. The most effective way to get people to follow you is to be the best shining example of who they themselves should emulate. If you want people to come in to work with a well maintained uniform but you come in a T-shirt and torn jeans, it's going to be significantly harder to persuade people. If you want people to work overtime but you're on the golf course 24/7, it's not happening. Especially for a young business looking to grow.

Another major factor involves getting everyone on your team to buy into your vision. Just because you have a clear vision of your company and where you want to take it doesn't mean that everyone else on the team is onboard with it. Besides communicating that vision, in order to get them on board you also have to *live it*. All of your actions need to be in line and congruent with the vision you espouse. Your team also needs to know why the vision is what it is and why they should care. You have to look at your team and think if you were in their shoes why should they buy into your master plan.

Erica Peitler: Leadership from the Ground Up

Erica Peitler left her role in a major pharmaceutical company to coach C-Suite executives on leadership skills. We got her views on how startup and early stage entrepreneurs can lead effectively.

According to Erica, the single most important quality/skill a new leader needs to succeed is to have a learning mindset, to recognize that learning is their ongoing job—one they will have to practice and hone over time. Erica advises young entrepreneurs to make sure their learning always has some structure to it. In a corporate environment, there are structured ways to learn but you have to provide the structure in the entrepreneurial field.

We couldn't help but ask, "Are there natural born leaders, or are leaders developed?" Erica responded, "It's always a blend; there are some natural things that leaders are hardwired with— many are charismatic, charming and easily build relationships, but it's really a skilled profession. Real leadership skills are built over time through practice. So-called natural leaders have to make this investment back into learning. They are hardwired, but over time they have to fill in the gaps in the skills that they have. For example, they need to be able to communicate a variety of things if pitching to a VC. They need to understand the decision making process." Erica emphasizes that it's all

learnable. However, she cautions that although there are some early advantages that give people a head start, that doesn't necessarily mean a strong finish.

Let's examine our leadership expert's advice for some Best Practices:

1. Make sure whatever you choose to do that you have some committed mentors invested in your success—being an entrepreneur doesn't mean being alone, even if it's just 1-2 people in the garage.

2. You have to know your hardwiring and which environment you will thrive in. If you don't have good focus, attention to detail and discipline, then you will not thrive as an entrepreneur. Or, bring in someone to cover your weaknesses. That said, the challenge is you have to be able to survive before you can bring someone on. An entrepreneur is going to take a risk and live in conditions with stress and challenges that others wouldn't choose to live with. Make sure the risk-reward equation is right for you. Make sure you're willing to put in the time, and that in the end it's worth it for you.

We asked our resident leadership expert Erica Peitler to define the difference between a good leader and a good manager. As you might guess, they are two totally different things. In Erica's words, "A good manager means getting things done right—driving efficiency, effectiveness; being task oriented. Good leadership involves making sure you're doing the right things, focusing on the stakeholders and making sure you have the resources to get things done."

The Most Common Leadership Mistakes to Avoid...

"When you start off you are really on your own and you become a jack of all trades. The trap is, as the organization grows, people often are slow and reluctant to let go and let other people do the work. Your capacity is limited by your own bandwidth and people don't often hand off roles fast enough. They are too slow to jump into the actual leadership role. They need to get to that next level so they are viewing their business at a higher altitude in order to see their next innovation for the company. Another one: mistakenly believing you're the smartest person in the room. As you bring people in, realize you are never as smart as the combined team. Don't fall in love with your own intelligence. It's really about bringing in more people and letting them feed off of your passion."

Visit Erica's website: www.ericapeitler. com read her blog posts and view her YouTube videos.

Chapter V

Become a Talent Scout

"You Cannot Teach a Man anything; You Can Only Help Him Find it Within Himself."

—*Galileo Galilei*

Fire the Haters (Hire for attitude, not for skills)

This turned out to be one of the best pieces of advice I got when it came to hiring. Why do I say this? Well, I had one employee who from day one always made known and emphasized his skills (in addition to his ability to beat his chest). He constantly drew attention to his ability to lift any piece, to get the job done efficiently, to make customers happy, to get great reviews and to have overall profitable days. So, what's wrong with that, you ask? These are all awesome things to do. However, there was one issue with this guy. His attitude was terrible. He used his ability as a basis to act superior to the rest of the team, and was totally ego driven. Furthermore, he was not at all a team player, and always took credit for everything that went well—and denied responsibility for anything that did not. This made it impossible for him to grow, as well. He thought he knew better than everyone else on the team...including the owner (moi), of course. Worst of all, he frequently complained and would belittle other employees and berate team mates he thought were underperforming. Most importantly though, was the effect of this sour attitude on the rest of the team. All of these attitude based issues not only upset the rest of the team, but also caused his mentality to spread to the rest of the team at times. Like any job, there are tough days. But, with a positive attitude, the majority of the guys on our crew would make the most of it and end up feeling good, nonetheless. However, whoever worked with him on a particular day would not end up with a positive attitude.

At first, I tolerated the attitude issues because he was my most profitable employee. However, when I understood the toll it was taking on the rest of the team, I realized that no amount of skills and ability is worth such a toxic attitude. Since then, it has always been our policy to hire on attitude over skills. Skills can be taught, but attitude is what makes a winning employee. So, how do we sniff out the (good smelling) attitude?

Our (very smart) hiring process is now designed to ferret out those traits right from the start. When talking to new hires, most of our interview questions are engineered to detemine how people behave and interact with other people, as opposed to just how much experience they have. I'll give ya a little of my secret sauce. *Here are some questions you can use:*

1. Tell me what makes a great team and give me a specific example of a time when you contributed to being part of a great team.
2. Give me a specific example of a time when you had to interact with some difficult people, and how did you make it work?
3. Did you ever have to carry more of the work load than someone else, and how did you handle that situation?
4. What does great customer service look like, and how have you delivered it in the past?

Finding Talent; the Deep Dive

Great people are all around you, but how do you find them? Well, I'll tell you how we do it. First, we work through our existing employees as much as possible. We have them share job listings through their social media networks, since they have tons of their own contacts. Second, I personally share the opportunity through all of my own contacts at networking events, and I have my business friends post it on their networks, as well. Why is this a better approach? Well, everyone coming to you has been pre-vetted, so there's less worry about their past. They come with built-in references that you can check before you even waste time going through the whole long, dragged out interview process—only to find out right before making the offer that something came up in their background check. (Axe murderers need not apply.) Also, people who are referring these candidates have a vested interest in only sending legitimate people. After all, it's a reflection on them. As for the employees referring people? The candidates hired will contribute to their (team's) work product, so they are inclined to only send the best people.

Today, times have changed. People are more sensitive and more guarded about who comes into their homes, so especially in home based service industries, you'll want to go through a meticulous process of both reference and background checking in order to know whom you are hiring. Sounds expensive? Not really, because you can use the quality of your vetting process as part of your marketing and sales message. Ultimately, the quality of your hires will affect the growth of the company, so it's critical to do a deep dive.

Developing and Grooming Talent

When hiring I screen for growth potential. I look for people who I think could one day become managers and one day own their own franchise or office. That way you're laying down the future of your company from

an early start. Once we hire someone, we have an extensive onboarding process. First, the employee has to do a physical challenge to show that he or she can do the actual work required. Then there's a group interview to screen for the first batch of people. Then there's a longer in person interview to select the best people from among them. When chosen, they begin a trial period where the actual work and their perfomance will determine if they're made an official offer. Finally, we have the whole team evaluate how well they do and if they're making a positive contribution to the quality of the team. We're not looking for people to just maintain the quality; we want them to bring it up. Only at that point do we make an official offer and bring someone on.

Once they begin work, that's when the real training starts. We establish a number of benchmarks right out of the gate to hit some early accomplishments, in order to keep them motivated and on target to become a manager—and to see who really *wants* to move up.

All the established workers take the newer members under their wing and develop them in all aspects of the business. You start off in our business as a "wing man" and then can get promoted to a "captain." In order to do so, we have a checklist of everything from knowing the vendors that we use, to how to work with customers, to how to have an efficient day and how to price accurately,

etc. We also do some role playing to practice before actually performing live. Still, it's always best to do the trial by fire and learn firsthand instead of just in a book. Experienced guys can critique the performance and keep developing the new hires every day until they can run their own trucks (real smart, right?)

While on the job training is the bedrock of what we do, it's also great to get outside perspectives from experts, so I encourage everyone on our team to read different books about business, marketing and personal development to keep growing and becoming a better person in general.

Since we've started, I've had a number of people who began with zero experience and are now leading the company and whole teams of people. Simply by taking their own initiative, many of them have even doubled their income.

Advice from the Barrister

We asked Kenneth Rosenberg, Esq., an employment attorney with Fox Rothschild LLP in Roseland, NJ, to help us navigate some of the choppiest waters you will encounter when you start to staff up. So, listen up and pay attention. This could save you a lot of headaches—and a lot of money. How do you know whether you can classify someone as an employee or as an independent contractor? (Hint: it's not worth trying to dodge the payroll taxes.) Let's take a look at a "short list" of the red flags the IRS looks for.

According to the IRS, the fundamental characteristic of an employment versus an independent contractor relationship is that the company has the right to control the manner and means by which the work is performed. The test used by the IRS to determine employment status for federal employment tax purposes is the common law right of control test. The relevant factors used to make this determination fall into the following three categories: (a) behavior controls, (b) financial controls and (c) type of relationship between the business and worker.

    A. Behavior Controls: The key factors in this category are whether the business retains the right to direct and control how the worker performs the specific tasks. An employee is generally subject to an employer's instructions regarding when, where and how to perform the

work. Providing training is one indication of employment status.

B. Financial Controls: The IRS will look to the following factors to determine whether the business retains the right to direct and control the financial aspects of the worker's activities: if the worker has unreimbursed business expenses; the worker's investment in his or her tools and equipment; if the worker's services are available to the marketplace; how the worker is paid; and the extent to which the worker can realize a profit or loss.

C. Type of Relationship: The following factors governing the relationship between the business and worker are significant in determining employment status:

(i.) whether there is a written contract with the worker;
(ii.) whether the business provides the worker with employee-type benefits, such as insurance, pension, vacation pay or sick pay;
(iii.) the permanency of the relationship; and
(iv.) the extent to which the worker's services are a key aspect of the regular business of the company.

49

If in doubt, consult a
qualified employment attorney.

Here's a minefield for some businesses. You want to be both politically and legally correct. But how do you differentiate between Gender & Age Discrimination and the ability to perform the necessary tasks of the job? For example, Junk-A-Haulics' business requires physically demanding work. Check out our expert's explanation.

Under Title VII, the ADEA and various state laws (such as the NJLAD) employers are prohibited from discriminating against applicants or employees based on their gender and age among other protected classifications. Accordingly, employers are prohibited from considering an individual's gender or age when making employment based decisions. Rather, the focus must be on the individual's ability to perform the duties of the job. The employer cannot assume that the individual cannot perform the duties of the job because of his/her gender or age. That is the very definition of discrimination.

There are a number of steps an employer can take to defend itself against accusations that it has engaged in gender or age discrimination when making employment decisions such as hiring/promotions/terminations where the job is physically demanding.

First, the employer should draft a detailed job description that accurately describes the minimum knowledge, skills and abilities required for the position and the essential and non-essential functions of the position. By doing so, it will be establishing the minimum requirements of the job which an employee must be able to perform.

Second, the employer should have a published Equal Employment Opportunity (EEO) policy which clearly states that the employer is committed to not discriminating against or harassing employees based on an individual's race, ethnicity, gender, age, religion or any other protected classification and provides equal employment opportunities when taking any employment based decisions such as hiring, promotions, terminations, compensation etc.

Third, the employer can use a short probationary period of 30-90 days to determine whether the employee is able to perform the job duties in a capable manner and indicate at the time of hire that he/she will be subject to successfully completing the probationary period. (Author's note: that's exactly what we do at Junk-A-Haulics.)

Fourth, if the position has demanding physical requirements and the employee indicates or the employer reasonably concludes the employee cannot perform the duties of the job,

job, it can send the employee for a fitness for duty exam based on the job description. If the employee fails the exam and is deemed unfit for the position the employer has a legitimate basis for terminating the employee.

Fifth, the employer should check the employee's references before making an offer to determine his prior work capabilities. This is not fail safe, as prior employers may not be forthcoming, but it could be a useful step in screening out poor candidates for the job.

Sixth, and perhaps most importantly, the employer should carefully document any and all examples of poor work which shows the individual cannot perform the duties of the job and thus had a legitimate business reason for terminating the employee.

Ultimately, while an employer cannot stop an individual from accusing it of engaging in illegal gender or age discrimination, if it takes the foregoing steps it can position itself to defend its legitimate business decision.

Sometimes you have a real good reason for firing someone. The lawyers call that "Termination with Cause." But, some people will try to sue, no matter what. So, how do you avoid employee lawsuits by documenting poor performance? Good, bad or otherwise, read what Attorney Ken Rosenberg from Fox Rothschild advises.

Employers that fairly, accurately and consistently document poor performance will be in a stronger position to defend against a baseless lawsuit because good documentation is the best evidence to show that an employee was not meeting its reasonable expectations and that it had legitimate business reasons to terminate the employee. Good rules of thumb in documenting poor performance include fairly evaluating performance, having witnesses corroborate poor performance of employees, consistently and timely documenting poor performance for all employees.

Chapter VI

Create a "WOW" Culture

"Our belief is That if You Get the Culture Right, Most of the Other Stuff—Like Great Customer Service, or Building a Great Long-Term Brand, or Passionate Employees and Customers—will Happen Naturally On its Own."

—Tony Hsieh

"The shared values of how the people work together to produce results and impact the world around them"

Let's start with our own personal definition of culture, okay? Culture involves the atmosphere— the climate of how people are feeling about the business. Culture includes how all the stakeholders (employees, owners and customers) interact with the business. It's the emotional component. So, where does a business's culture come from? It's an outgrowth of the founders' passion communicated through the organization. The culture encompasses the shared values of how the people work together to produce results and impact the world around them. The product or service that the company delivers is its function, but its culture is the feeling that its people get working there and the customers feel doing business with the company.

Ask yourself these questions: What makes for a healthy and positive culture? What can negatively impact your culture? Who owns the culture? Let's poke around here. Early on in our company, I thought we had a good culture because I had very positive feelings about it. However, what I realized early was that as we grew from just myself to a whole team, my perception of the culture was not shared by all parties. One of the main issues was that I was so focused on growing the company and keeping the lights on that I neglected to see how all the other people in the company felt simply coming to work everyday. (That could be stupid.)

The first major issue was that we started with a separate office and warehouse. This was due to financial reasons, but I gradually noticed the effects of having the management in one place and the haulers in another. Our team cameraderie was killed when the guys running it and the guys on the trucks were not together and able to interact. Furthermore, all you needed was one person with a negative attitude. Since I wasn't there to defuse the situation, it became very easy for that person to spread their negativity to others. After making the switch to a unified office and warehouse I noticed our culture became impacted greatly in a positive way. It gave me the opportunity to take a closer look and really see what was going on with everyone.

Simply put, a healthy culture would be one where everyone working there buys into the mission of the company. They all feel empowered and motivated. They feel like they own a stake in the company, and what happens to it matters to them. It takes a pro-active effort. You need to have activities for team building. You must show appreciation. At the very basic level people just want to know that their work is valued and it matters. It's not hard, it's not expensive; it's simply a matter of caring and valuing your people—and showing it. A healthy culture has core values that the company, its management and its employees live by. Each culture can vary based on the industry, but it reflects and and echoes down through the employees, the product or service, and the company's relationship with its customers and the community.

It's key to show employees they're valuable through promoting things like work life balance, like having a gym or getting good rates to a place to help with their fitness, or programs to help with babysitting if they have kids. Having happy hours – a place to socialize outside of work to start viewing people you work with as more than just co-workers pays big dividends. Some people have an old school mentality of strict boundaries between their personal and professional life, but the reality today is that that distinction is pretty blurry and it should be—because employees who view the people they work with as their second family are going to be way more productive and happy at work. (Definitely smart.)

So, who owns the culture? Well the founder/CEO is responsible for setting it and putting the framework in place, but the employees are responsible for taking ownership of it, for perpetuating it and passing it on to new hires. You can spot a bad culture a mile away. It's the one without the right incentives in place, whereby people are motivated. In the movie *Office Space,* the main character Peter says to "the Bobs," a pair of corporate "layoff specialists," how he really has no incentive to work any harder or any more than the bare minimum because there's no rewards for doing so. And furthermore, he mentions how he has 8 bosses who barely know who he is and all tell him the same things when something goes wrong.

Bad cultures are impersonal. You are employee 3457 – people don't know your name, your interests, your family, or your talents. Bad cultures are toxic to your business. They lead to high employee and customer turnover, which is one of the most expensive things a business can have to deal with. Bad cultures promote internal cut throat competition—where everyone claws to get ahead of other people and don't support the rise of everyone, but rather just their own myopic success. These are the people who wouldn't do a favor for you or cover for you when you needed, or would steal a client from you or step on your toes. That kind of environment makes people even afraid to approach their co-workers for anything. While you might get short term gains from a cut throat atmosphere like this, ultimately you're getting a substandard product because people are always stronger working together and building on collective strengths to get everyone to the next level.

Typically, bad cultures are run by management acting with negative reinforcement—the fear factors rules. A boss who continually makes you feel like your job is always on the line, like you're never good enough, if you slip up you never hear the end of it—as opposed to one who allows people to fail and learn from mistakes, and emphasizes when they do good to make them feel like they're making progress and help them identify and build on their strengths.

Your hiring process is a key factor to find people who match your culture right out of the gate. You need to take the core values that your company operates on and all your hiring and firing decisions need to be made based on that. For example, one of our values is "teamwork makes dreamwork". It's all about the individuals on the team having no ego. Now this can be tricky though. We try our best to screen for this first off – looking for people who are confident but not overly boastful of their past successes. It's subtle things that you might not pick up without really looking for it, which is why it needs to be a key element in the screening process. Sometimes people are good actors and can slip through, but in that case you need to give them a chance. But if they don't change their ways you need to be very principled when it comes to enforcing those values if you ever really want a culture genuinely aligned with your vision. That includes letting people go when they don't uphold those values. The no ego clause can be challenging on this end, too because the people with bigger egos usually come from your top performers. If you have lesser performance you're not about to go bragging about it. But it's those top performers that sometimes lead to some very difficult choices when you have to part with those people; even though they might be big money makers, it's not worth the detriment to your culture. You must consider all the other people who work for you and how it impacts them.

Getting to the Core of the Matter

So, here's my (smart, not stupid) take on promoting a great culture in your young, growing company: It starts with your core values. How do you set them? For starters, pick between 3-5 core values. Don't pick more; otherwise it will dilute them or diminish the importance of them. If you have 10 core values then it's hard to prioritize and reinforce all of them to the same extent. Because you can only pick a small number of values they should be multi-dimensional. For example, a good value and one of our Core Values is "Ownership Mentality." The reason why this is very effective is because it permeates all aspects of the business—it encourages our haulers to own up to mistakes made and correct them, and on our management team it holds us accountable to decisions we make on the strategic level and it doesn't let anyone pass the buck. It can be further used to encourage everyone to treat the company like it's their own and to not bring problems, but rather bring us solutions.

I always advocate learning from the masters. (Yes, they're smart.) When it comes to developing your core values, take your cues from Verne Harnish, author of *Scaling Up*. Here's his advice:

Your core values should not just be a single word like honesty or integrity because those are basically just platitudes that are so ubiquitous and ill defined that they're rendered meaningless. Instead, he suggests using phrases that also communicate your company's personality. The core values should be very intertwined with the feel and experience of your company's culture.

In his own words:

"Core Values are the rules and boundaries that define the company's culture and personality, and provide a final 'Should/Shouldn't' test for all the behaviors and decisions by everyone in the firm."[3]

As Verne Harnish relates in *Scaling Up*, Core Values also help with delegation because if someone on the leadership team assigns a task to an employee and the employee has a tricky decision to make, he can refer to the Core Values to figure out what the leadership would say. Lastly there are two great questions you can ask to help identify those values which are, "What is the BEHAVIOR" that comes out of this Value? This can help you identify exactly what it should LOOK like, which helps to determine the Value and for the team to understand it better. And also think about what questions you would ask a prospective employee—or even a current one to determine if they would or do live by those specific values.

People and Profit: Inseparable

Let's look at how companies are creating and promulgating their cultures in today's business world. Silicon Valley attracted the best talent by offering great perks like free transportation, housing, onsite lunches. They offered things that spoke to the younger generation that wasn't just focused on the money. It was about how it felt to be a part of those

---

[3] *Scaling Up; How a Few Companies Make it, and Why the Rest Don't,* ©Gazelles, LLC

teams and organizations. The ultimate benefit gained by attracting the best talent? The company knew that it would achieve greater profitability. They were investing in people. They placed a high value on human capital. This is a distinguishing factor of newer companies appealing to a younger demographic. Let's look at an example. "Zappos is a customer service company that just happens to sell shoes." -Tony Hsieh (from the founder's book *Delivering Happiness*). Rule of thumb: treat your employees with the same level of quality that you do for your customers. Look at Google. When I visited their offices in New York City, they actually had a slide in the middle of the office. Play was just as important as work. One of my favorite things that I saw is that they had two different kinds of food jars. The clear one had the healthy snacks and the opaque ones had the unhealthy but delicious snacks. The perks also extend past just fun convenience things. At Google they take frequent days where you can basically become your own inventor. You can work on whatever project you want, regardless of whether it's in your department, and submit the ideas to the guys on top. Numerous services from Google have been invented by people not even responsible for performing those roles. Notice how the tech companies have more open office environments – less of a silo culture fosters more collaboration. The CEO often sits at a desk right next to everyone else. No closed door offices; this marks a major shift with the youthpreneur generation.

Some sales companies offer cruises to their top performers. Look at a company and look at its lunch room and you get a window into their culture. If the management is sitting with the employees, you get the feeling how the people interact there. Richard Branson's company offers unlimited vacation. Now, you still have to get your work done; the idea is simply that if you can hit all your objectives, but you can do it more efficiently or on your own terms, then by all means, do so. They are empowering the people to live their lives how they want to without all the traditional corporate limitations and outdated ways of thinking. Some companies even offer massages to their workers—how nice is that!

Culture, while an internal attribute, also relates to the production and delivery of the work product serving the customer and the community. By encouraging a positive, vibrant internal employee culture, you can see it right away when speaking with someone at the company. If you call in on the phone, we all know those big behemoth bloated companies when you talk to customer service and you can feel their disdain for working there and perhaps even talking to you. Or they try their best to cover it up, but you can always tell—or worse yet, they've outsourced it. Then you can tell the people really don't care because they're not even part of the company. (Destined to produce stupid results.)

In contrast, it's very apparent when the people are so friendly you can tell they are happy to be there and want to talk with you because they are passionate and believe in their company's product or service. They not only take their job seriously, but they want to help you come up with a solution. Here's a real world example of that principle in action. An individual purchased an Apple® product and had a problem with it. He called customer service;

they checked his social media profile, noticed that he had a large following and immediately offered to replace the product with no questions asked for free, because they understood the impact of a happy influential customer versus an unhappy influential customer. This would not have happened in many older type companies. Take Starbucks®, who pays for their full-time employees' health benefits—very unique for its industry, and this draws a lot of people in; for that level job it's a rare practice.

Apple employees at their retail stores don't get paid commissions, but receive a higher salary instead. Now, it can be a risky move doing so, because then in theory it's easier to just coast by and not sell as many products. But by hiring people who seem to have a genuine passion for the work and the company, the benefit is greater because it creates a less cut throat culture and one that emphasizes all the team members to work together to improve the customers' experience in the store as a whole. (Very smart indeed.)

Great culture is not necessarily limited to new companies. It's all about the empowerment of the employees. For example, an employee of TD Bank authored a book about her sister-in-law's battle with cancer and the bank threw an elaborate catered open house to help her sell the book and raise funds for alterative treatment therapies. Even though TD bank is an older, more established place, the fact that their managers at the local level felt comfortable enough to do this means that the culture throughout the whole organization must be geared towards this kind of mentality and spirit.

Here's a little more of our story in building our own Junk-A-Haulics company culture. As I mentioned at the start of this chapter, we had the issue with the separate office and warehouse. First, because the guys couldn't see me on a daily basis, they would assume I was on a beach in Bermuda sipping margaritas while they toiled away. We fixed this by leasing a larger combined office/warehouse in one location. Now, with that change, when they'd come back from their hard day they'd be able to see me burning the midnight oil and working hard into the night, which set the right tone and helped them to see the bigger picture. The new space also allowed us to chat after work and see how their day went, get their pulse on how they're feeling about the company and address those matters EARLY before they become something larger that we could easily fix earlier. And of course, have fun! We now have in our office a pool table, a ping pong table, a dart board, a beer fridge (for after work, of course!), an old school N64 console with all the games, movie theater chairs and a big screen TV, plenty of places to hang out, a cigar area, a full gym and even a basketball hoop! At the end of a hard day hauling junk, what better way to unwind then a quick game of ping pong with your boss? It really does wonders to put everyone on the same level and show that we can all have fun together as well as work together.

It's fun to be able to beat your boss in a game of ping pong or pool, but it's even more fun to watch them flop around in the mud. On one team outing we joined a Tough Mudder 10 mile obstacle course through lots and lots of mud. On top of that, the day that we did it there was a heavy downpour, so everything was a massive mud fest and they got to see me get thrown around in the mud, we helped pull each other up muddy walls and wade through quick flowing muddy rivers. Afterwards, they were treated to a big steak dinner and some beers. Doing events like that where you really have to work together as a team can do wonders for cameraderie and really show that they are part of something special. Which is all people really want in the first place. (Nothing stupid about that!)

Also, part of the culture involves giving back. We donate to lots of great charities when we can. One of our favorites is Habitat Restore, a division of Habitat For Humanity. All the proceeds from the sale of second hand furniture in their store goes to help build homes. It's a charity I'm very passionate about. By focusing on this too, we create a general spirit of contributing to the community and everyone takes part in it together. This creates our shared mindset and aligns our values so that we're all operating on the same level. Internally, these values and experiences translate into an external experience for the customer. Because internally we are focused on having fun, working hard in unison together as a team, fostering a sense of cameraderie, the customer can feel these things when we're working at a job. For example, if we send two guys out on a job—instead of typical contractors barking at each other to do this and do that, our guys are joking around with each other and the customer. They are genuinely interested in serving the customer's needs and going the extra mile to deliver a truly fantastic experience. They do this day in and day out because they enjoy working with the company, and customer service then becomes a natural outgrowth of their pride in the company.

Chapter VII

The Power of Intuition

"Ignoring Intuition is Like Touching a Hot Stove: You Need Only Get Burned Once to Know That Ignoring Your Intuition is NOT a Good Idea."

—A. Artemis

Get in Touch With It

Think back—way back, to the arrival of our species on this rock we fondly call earth. When we grunted and groaned—yes, that far back. Intuition: this is our primal self. Before there was knowledge, there was intuition. This is how we survived. (What, no Monday night football?) Our intuition guided us to avoid danger in all its many forms. Intuition was innate in our primitive self. Intuition knows what to do. It always has. It ain't stupid. Fast forward through the millenia. We all still have it. It's buried deep within us. Often, we don't know how to tap into it.

Children use their intuition more than adults do. Think back (not so far, this time; hold it right there). As a child, you were taught to think before you act—not to be impulsive. Our teachings socialized the intuition out of us in certain ways. As a result, we as adults then suffer from over-analysis—or paralysis through analysis, as many call it.

"We Suppress Our Intuition When It's Often Correct"

Make no mistake, this stuff is powerful. Intuition is like the genie in the bottle (but you're not limited to three wishes). The power of intuition amounts to this: often times we instincively know what needs to be done, yet we complicate the decision process and suppress our intuition. We don't pay enough attention to it, but it's often correct. So, when does this powerful force come into play? More often than you might realize. Intuition stealthily sneaks its way into the hiring process, into customer relations and into your interactions with your employees. It simply works at the unconscious level, so we remain unaware of it.

So, how do we get in touch with it? (email, fax, text, cell phone? I don't think so.) I find myself using my intuition when making decisions in a number of business situations. You use your intuition when you know to walk away from a customer that is not a good fit for your business. When hiring employees, I sometimes failed to follow my intuitive sense when I knew certain people were under performing. I knew I wasn't happy about it, but I didn't acknowledge my instinct. It was there and I was pushing it aside. (That could be stupid.)

On the other hand, I found intuition proved useful in business. When I began to explore entering my business, I wanted to jump right in. Then I found out that it took a year and a half to get the license—and I could not operate for that entire time. On paper, it amounted to a really bad proposition: you had to shell out a bunch of money, wait a super long time and put your entire life on hold during some drawn out bureautcratic process. But, intuitively, I felt this was the right move. At the time, a number of people thought I was just plain nuts for banking everything on basically being a garbage man, but I knew it was the right move. (And there are some pretty rich garbage men out there, ya know). So, it's not like I'm advocating for imprudence or illogical, emotionally driven thought. There was actually a foundation of reasoning, but when it came time to pull the trigger, it was intuition that saw me through that—and I'm glad it did.

"Intuition Keeps You Aligned With Your Value System"

Here's another critical piece to this puzzle. Consider this. How does intuition play into your value system? Well, for me, in the junk hauling business, I truly believe we are improving people's lives by removing their clutter, by helping the environment through recycling and by re-purposing older items that needy people can use. Intuition plays into our values on a more basic level. We want to be in a business that aligns with our value system. So, I guess my intuition guided me to a decision that amounted to a lot more than being a garbage man.

Intuition: How and When to Use It

The big question then for all of us: how do we access and connect with our intuition? I admit. I do it in the shower.

When you are relaxed and doing something that doesn't require a lot of concentration—the more mundane the task, the better—that's when you increase the chance that your mind can "wander without intention". Here's how it works. Often, you'll simply stumble upon some great ideas or solve a problem. If we try to force outcomes, often we can go further astray. It happens late at night or early in the morning, outside of business hours and family time—when you're totally disconnected, with no social media or emails. Eliminate the distractions and find your quietest times. A lot of my best ideas crystalize simply through talking with people. When you free associate, someone gives you a thought and all the relevant connections to it arise...and sometimes the answer reveals itself.

What do you do when that stuff comes up? I write down everything. Absolutely everything. I do this first of all because it's hard to sit down and come up with great ideas on command. Most of my reasonably good ideas come spontaneously when I'm doing something else, so I always make sure to capture them when I can. When I first did this I would end up with far too much information to do anything with, so once a week I'll take my notes and distill the best points and move them to the top of my thought list and tasks list. This stuff then flows into my business plans and more strategic logic-based thinking. The two work hand in hand and connections often arise from the merger of the two types of thinking.

Did I ever go back and compare intuitive stuff with logical stuff? Yes. Were there times when I did over analyze or I should have just gone with my first instinct? Yes, again. There were big decisions relating to the growing pains in my business. Nine months into the business, I had to decide whether or not to buy a second truck. Early on, there was the decision to hire my first hauler; later, the decison to promote the first person. I had a trademark issue and had to decide whether I call the person to settle the issue or to hire an attorney. Then came the big one—moving into this big space. So, let's look at how I handled a few of these.

"Sometimes You Have to Take Some Risks and Go With Your Gut"

One of the biggest decisions I had to make early on was whether to purchase a second truck when I was only 9 months into the business. Now logically, I did not yet have the need for that truck to be hauling full time. Like much of the early years in running a business, money was tight and I had already increased some of our other expenses. So on paper it didn't necessarily look like a good idea. However, my instincts were telling me that the way business was going, the only way we were going to be able to grow and meet potential demand was to buy that truck. Because we were at such an early stage in the business, I didn't do formal projections of what our revenues would be. Frankly those are often very speculative anyway. Ultimately I decided to go for it, and I'm very glad I did. Without it, we would have had to turn down a lot of business and we wouldn't have had nearly the success we did that first year. What does that say about this process or about growing your business? Sometimes you have to take some risks and go with your gut. (You just have to have a smart gut!) Really, it's not reckless. I knew there was potential business out there. I knew I would work twice as hard to keep that truck on the road if I now had access to it. The goal of winning more business really just manifested itself as a truck. This is what entrepreneurship is all about.

One of my heros of advocating intuition is Richard Branson. When he first launced his airline, Virign Atlantic, he didn't do a bunch of market research to determine the viability of another airline in the mix. And frankly, if he did that research he probably wouldn't have gone for it because Britsh Airways at the time was a massively dominant player. Plus, there were a lot of anti-competitive practices in the market at the time that almost pushed him out of business numerous times. But he just went for it based on the fact that he could plainly see the need for a better customer experience while flying. Instead of looking at operations, his decision to launch was driven by the customer experience, which is a way more intuitive approach.

"Intuition can Drive Profits Just as Much as Spreadsheets Can"

Here's another great example of intuitive thinking driving a business. Tom's Shoes – when you buy a pair of shoes, they send one to people in need. Again, if his accountant saw that model he'd probably have a heart attack. But the owner of Tom's knew instinctively that people who shared that value would line up in droves to purchase his products...and purchase they did. Intuition can drive profit just as much as spreadsheets can.

Chapter VIII

Time Marches On

"If You Have More Than Three Priorities, You Don't Have Any."

—*Jim Collins*

Mastering Time Management

Let me tell you about my earliest lessons in time management before I really understood and applied any real degree of time management to my life and to my business. To be really dead honest, time management was not something I learned early on. I didn't feel like I had a natural ability to do it and nobody ever made a point of it to me. It was mostly just emphasized to work really hard and to get everything done, as opposed to working smarter and more efficiently.

Focus = Priorities + Deadlines

I heard the word "focus" tossed around my whole life. I always just thought it was another vapid/well intentioned but meaningless word. Then, at one point I finally understood the real mechanics/components of how you can actually implement more focus in your day. Yes, I had the "aha!" moment. I had this realization chatting at a bar with someone randomly, of all places. They made the point that all the most successful organizations have an extreme amount of focus in every area of their business. As we chatted on I realized that, in order to have focus, there are really two key areas. The first is another overused and not well defined word, prioritization. I always understood the dictionary definition but I never realized its true importance and how to implement it. The second is deadlines, a word that I used to loathe in college. Why? Because I would frequently ask my professors for extensions! I now love deadlines and, as I eventually learned, they are essential to running a successful organization.

Deadlines Are Do or Die

In order to get focused you need to set rock solid priorities and deadlines. Focus is synonymous with prioritization and deadlines. As I mentioned from my college days, I remember there was one time where I had to turn in a paper by 5PM on a particular day. I arrived at 5:05PM to drop it off and the professor said, "Sorry, I cannot accept that; it's after the deadline." I was outraged, and from that point on I despised the word "deadlines." However, in my later years I have come around

"Deadlines Keep Getting You Closer to Where You Want to Be"

quite a lot. Deadlines become something to reach for instead of an obstacle. Consider this analogy—deadlines are like climbing a rope ladder; you keep reaching for the next rung, and each rung (or deadline) is getting you one step closer to where you want to be. There is something almost magical about them because deadlines keep you on track. Remember cramming for an exam the night before, or pulling an all nighter working on a month long paper that you're now burning the midnight oil around the clock to finish? Well, we all had a month to get that paper done but we wound up doing it in a day or two anyway. Instead of fighting who you are (old habits die hard!), why not just work with that.? Here's how: by setting up a bunch of mini "do or die" deadlines you ensure that what you really need to get done doesn't get pushed off or delayed. Since you've already identified it as a priority (in the first step) you now make sure that it actually gets done and done when you need it to be done.

Think about this: in the stock market, things happen in milliseconds and everything changes rapidly. If you had an order to submit for your client and you didn't get it through in time, then the value of their portfolio drops. Consider the impact of missing a deadline—it's not just a deadline because I said it is. The world, and the business world in particular, runs on deadlines. If you don't meet your client's deadline, then you probably won't have the client any more. Deadlines are not arbitrary. They're there because you have a mission and each large project is a sum of many smaller actions; if you have one massive project and don't put a time stamp on it, then it's extremely easy to keep pushing it off and off and off without even realizing it. Meanwhile, most people do that because those are the long term (non urgent but very important) tasks they think can wait because they're putting out fires. But those long term projects are the ones that really push the business forward and grow it.

So, even though at the time I resented my professor for doing that, I now appreciate why he did it. It was because deadlines were sacred to him. You have to treat them like that and never break them. The reason why self imposed deadlines are so effective is because that's how you keep yourself accountable. Somebody else (namely your client) is depending on you, and if you don't meet their deadlines then they lose and you lose. What if you were selling life insurance and the client dies but you didn't submit the policy paperwork on time? Now *that's* do or die! It's a level of commitment you make to them, and it is reflected in your personal deadlines and other people's deadlines you must meet. And most of all, remember to treat your appointments with yourself like you treat those with your cleints. Never break a deadline that you commit to yourself to do. At the same time, there are self imposed deadlines that, by reaching for the deadlines, even if you don't fully achieve them on time, at least they got you started and on track. There are times where even if you don't exactly hit the mark, it's okay (particularly if it's a slightly lower priority). Clients' deadlines obviously have to be met, but there are times with self imposed deadlines where even though we want to treat them as do or die, at the same time you don't want to beat yourself up if you didn't meet one—as long as you set the deadline, worked towards it and at least came close.

The two most important planning deadlines that I personally set are the 90 day (i.e. quarterly project deadlines) and the weekly deadlines. The idea behind the 90 day deadlines is that you can step back and at a glance, look at everything that you want to get done that quarter to move your company forward. 90 days is a very managable amount of time, as opposed to a year, which is way too far out to list all the projects you have. Or a month, which can get eaten up by just a small number of projects. Each week I scan the 90 day master list of projects and key objectives and pull out 3-5 key tasks for that week, put it onto 1 sheet of paper and then post it somewhere next to my desk very visibly. All week I know that it doesn't matter where, when or how I get those done, but I can't end the week until they are accomplished. If you're a solo-preneur and want to keep yourself accountable, then that sheet of paper can do the trick. When other fires to put out and papers fly across your desk, you can always look back at that to remember that you have until the end of the week to get those tasks done. You may have to push aside a less important email or phone call because you are committed to hitting your deadlines. If you do have employees (and even better, if you have a mangement team), then it is extremely helpful sharing those objectives with your team Monday morning and then doing a recap on Friday, because we all know we'd never want to disappoint someone we made a commitment to. This is also a smart, useful system to hold your employees to as well. It's mutual accountability across the board. In summary, priorities are critical to focus because they narrow down the scope to only the most essential actions (hence blocking out unecessary distractions and non-ROI generating activites), and when you're working towards a deadline you get a kind of tunnel vision where you have a single minded attention on the task at hand and actually seeing it through to fruition.

Keep our formula top of mind: **focus= priorities + discipline**. This is above all the number one thing to remember when it comes to time management. That said, there are of course many other tips and tricks out there that can also help. We'll lay some on you later in the chapter.

My first real exposure to the principles of time management came when I entered the financial arena. I was fresh out of school, very ambitious (and a little naive! but not stupid) and ran up against this issue in full force, wanting to do everything. All of that changed with a simple quotation, which was "That Which Matters Most Must Never Be At The Mercy of That Which Matters Least" – Goethe. So German playwrites are typically not people's first stop for work efficiency, but when I heard this quotation everything kind of made sense to me regarding time management. What I realized was happening was that throughout my entire life I was under the assumption that if I just worked harder and for longer hours, then I could accomplish everything. Not a crazy assumption but a flawed one, because we can come up with enough work to occupy 5 people if we wanted to, but that is simply not feasible. What also really clicked about this quotation, was the fact that I was actually sacrificing certain objectives which would make a huge impact on my business and my life at the cost of trying to accomplish tasks of much lesser value.

One of the most challenging things about this process though, is that everything FEELS important, especially in the moment. I typically capture all my tasks onto one document and then I'll go in later and prioritize them from there. However, most time management books advocate that you list your tasks as A, B or C, or High Value, Medium Value or Low Value. However, if something was important enough for you to write it down, chances are that you're not writing down a ton of unimportant things. When I tried that system I struggled with it because I still wound up putting nearly all my tasks in the top category. So I changed those classifications to Extremely Important, Very Important, Important. And if it wasn't important then I would just remove the tasks altogether. I try to comb through and make sure my task list priorities are accurately reflected on a weekly basis. "If you have more than 3 priorities then you have none" – Jim Collins - "Feeling overwhelmed is really just a lack of priorities" – Jim Collins – These are so true. When you clarify your priorities and limit them, your stress melts away.

By implementing this system, I've had a tremendous increase not just in productivity but in mental sanity. My mind is more at rest and relaxed knowing that the handful of objectives that really matter and will make a signficant impact on my business and life are in a small, very managable category, so that I can just look there instead of at the entire list. If I have 100 things on my task list but I know that there are really only 5-10 that absolutely must get done, then a giant weight is lifted off my shoulders. At first, I was worried about not getting to the items in the other tiers, but that's not the right way to look at it. Now I still aspire to get through as many tasks as I can; however, I don't worry about the other levels until I get the "Extremely Important" tasks done first.

For example, in addition to the mental clutter issue that I had before implementing this strategy, I was also at times letting things slip through the cracks—or I would realize that I had to get something done the day before and would have to scramble at the last minute to get it done because it would get lost in the mass of tasks. (Not smart.) After implementing this system, I was able to cut back on my hours and accomplish more in less time. It's not about working harder and longer; it's about working smarter and more strategically.

As a child of an immigrant, I was instilled with a tremendous sense of work ethic that has been invaluable to my success. However, some of the strategic thinking is a lot of times not passed on, as in my case. So, although not an expert, I am now somewhat accomplished in this area and happy to share what works. So, notepads, ipads, shoulder pads—write it down wherever you'll see it. Here's Junkman Jeff's guidelines for successful (not stupid) time mangagement:

A. You're key activities should always be revenue generation or ROI based
B. Schedule appointments back to back when I can and schedule them around meals when I'm going to be taking time for that anyway
C. Offensive Time vs. Defensive time: This is a lesson I learned early on in sales. The key hours for selling or talking to prospects are usually

around 9AM-4PM, so you should spend that time solely focused on either meeting with clients or calling them to set the appointment. You don't want to waste time doing other activities during this time. That said, being organized, planning and your other tasks are still important, but they are best done on off-peak hours like 7AM-9AM or after 4PM.

D. Choose wisely WHOM you spend your time with

E. Keep all tasks consolidated in one form—not a few things on Post-it® notes, a few things on your phone, a few things on word docs on your computer, a few on bits of paper or notecards – then that challenges the integrity of the system.

F. Break down large massive projects into very small bite sized chunks and attach a time frame to each (i.e. set deadlines for yourself). Live your life by self imposed deadlines. By setting and sticking to your own mini-deadlines, you can get more accomplished.

G. Set dedicated times for email and returning calls, so as not to interrupt work flow

H. David Allen, the productivity guru, coined the 2 minute rule—any project that can take under 2 minutes is best to just bang it out and be done with it instead of spending 2 minutes just to write it down, only to waste more time addressing it later.

I. Cross it off rule! This one is very simple but a very important one. When making task lists it is very defeating when you just keep adding items to the list without crossing them off. Crossing off the task is very satisfying because you get the sense of accomplishment that you're making progess, which in turn gives you energy and momentum to get to the next stage.

J. And of course, one step at a time! I'll admit it this one seems so simple, but it is something you always have to keep in mind. If you look at a list of stuff to do it's easy to get overwhelmed and not know where to start. You have to always bring your attention back to the first step in the project and just knock each one off one at a time. Then you will feel way less overwhelmed and can methodically and calmly move towards your goal.

Chapter IX

Understanding Technology

"Everything Should Be Made As Simple As Possible, But Not Simpler."

—Albert Einstein

Making it Work For You...and Avoiding Tech Traps

When I first started my company, I had to schedule all the appointments coming in. Technology was great for being able to store all that information on a mini-computer in my pocket—commonly called a smart phone. (There's a reason they call it that.) Unfortunately however, in the first few months technology was not working for me because when job info came in I would put it in all different places. I would put some info in the calender, some info in the digital notepad, other info in an email I would send to myself and sometimes I would even revert back to paper (heavens, do they still make that?) because I had now made my digital notes a mess. I realized this simply wasn't working when my notes became so jumbled that I lost track of my jobs altogether.

At one point, I had an appointment scheduled and I had the guy's name and work order, but no address! (Really stupid.) It was then that I decided that something had to change.

In order to fix it, I looked at the 5 or so current places where I was taking down notes and figured out which one would be the best long term strategy for running a smoothly operating and organized business; I realized this was the electronic calender. The only problem with the calendar on my phone was that as I scaled the business, none of my employees could see my calendar anymore. There are a lot of costly high tech solutions out there, but I did some research into other options and found that Google® Calender can very easily be shared within an organization. This allowed not only me, but also my managers later on, to edit the calender without any headaches. The great thing about this program is that everything is automatically backed up to the cloud and it auto-saves literally every 2 seconds, so you don't even have to save your work. How smart is that?

"You Can Run Your Entire Operation All from Wireless Devices"

Jeff's Brainstorm: for a small start up and early stage business, one of the great things is that you don't need expansive and expensive hardwired systems. In many fields, you can run your entire operation all from wireless devices such as laptops, tablets and phones. Three years into the business and 10 employees later, it still works great for us. Let's dive a little deeper into the tech pool.

iPads®: Personally, I never understood the point of iPads. (Does that make me stupid? Just asking.) About 3 years after they first came out I finally caved in and bought one for personal use because everyone seemed to think they were great. I used it for about a month and then let it sit on my shelf for the next few years. At some point though, I thought about how it could be used for business and then came up with a multitude of excellent uses. First, instead of going to job sites with a bag stuffed full of papers to write estimates and take notes with my terrible handwriting, we can now make very professional looking estimates and email them on the spot. Our workers were able to take credit cards right on the jobsite with a screen large enough for all of our customers to read easily, which then improved cash flow by getting immediate payment. Furthermore, now that everyone always has a camera (since it's built into the iPad) we are now able to better document jobs and take photos of the jobs all the time for social media. (Yes, even selfies!) The abundance of photos helped the quality of our social media 10 fold and led to a good amount of business later.

One of our biggest challenges prior to getting iPads was getting online reviews. Often times we would inform our customers at the end of jobs that they could review us online, but it didn't happen because by the time we left, they got distracted. Now with iPads we've been able to simply hand the device directly to the customer and get the review on the spot. We now use a program that automatically texts a link to the customers' phones so they can very easily leave a review for us with just one click. Doing this one simple trick has more than doubled our reviews and led to an increase in business.

Quickbooks™ Online - This tool is a great help. You get all the updates as they come out, my bookkeeper can work remotely and for the first few months I was even able to do it by myself. Brace yourself—here comes the big one...

"I Set Up My Entire Business On Google Completely for Free"

Google: Google is way more than search. I basically set up my entire business on Google completely for free. First I registered my domain name on Google. Using a program called Google Apps I was able to integrate their email and calender platform for not just myself, but for my entire team—again, *at no cost*. We set up Google Docs so that myself and all of our employees could access, share and collaborate on text documents, slideshow presentations and excel documents, all while making edits simultaneously. It goes even further. Google even has a free telephone system allowing you to use your cell phones, but having people call a business number. There are some more robust systems that are good for larger organizations, but for a free service Google Voice worked wonders for us. For marketing campaigns and market research we were able to use Google Trends to see what people were searching for, so that we could optimize our SEO. We used Google Analytics to monitor how we were aquiring customers onto our website and even follow their behavior on the site. Eventually, when we decided to finally pay Google for advertising, we used their Adwords software to run and analyze campaigns to make sure we were converting the greatest number of people to paying customers. This is only a fraction of the products that Google offers, but all of these helped our business tremendously; we can't wait to see what they come out with next!

Social Media, love it or hate it; everything about it has already been written before and emphasized to death. The one thing that can't be emphasized enough however, is the importance of pictures. Just look at the trends now, taking Buzzfeed as an example. People don't want to read essays online...especially if it's just a company they are following. They ALSO don't want generic crap. No one is dying to read some third party article about planting flowers or what you ate for lunch. If you're going to post stuff, make it meaningful, relevant and useful—but most of all it should be a candid portrayal of your company's culture, and the best way to reflect that is through pictures. We never sell on social media. We either educate or simply show photos of all the cool things we're doing or seeing that benefit others. That is the best and arguably one of the only ways to have an effective social media campaign. The only thing that rivals (or maybe exceeds) pictures is video. This often takes more work to get done, but the investment is worth it because video is extremely engaging and effective, and now highly searchable. Google bought YouTube, making YouTube the number 2 search engine on the planet. Therefore your web presence is blind to the number 2 search engine without video.

Your Website: Websites are obviously a mandatory thing to have in business today. However, you don't have to spend a fortune. First decide what kind of functionality the site needs. Is it just a brochure online or does it need to have very robust functionality; such as taking orders, scheduling appointments, capturing data, etc? For a lot of businesses, it is simply a brochure online. If that's the case there are a number of web designers who can get that done very cost effectively. That said, if you're not a designer don't try this at home. A small investment is worth the huge dividends it will pay later. Also, a great website doesn't have to be a very involved one. For my first website, I went for a very clean minimalistic look which cost very little, but I still got a number of compliments on the site because it was clutter free (like us!) and easy to navigate without lots of distractions. If your website is built on WordPress® for example, it is very upgradable, like a lot of similar platforms out there. Crawl, before you walk before you run, baby!

"Pay Attention to Your Whole Online Presence, Not Just Your Website"

You need to pay attention to your whole online presence, not just your website. It's all your video channels, social media, PR articles and other things that come up in online searches— and can back link, sending peope to your site. Remember, it's about having more content about your business in more places online. People may not know your company name or your website domain name, but if they search for your subject matter, you want to be sure they find you.

Your Logo: There are also inventive websites to help you get logos and other creative work done inexpensively. One of them is 99designs.com, which was a life saver when I started my company. When I first started I knew I needed a logo and I knew the importance of having an awesome one, but I was having difficulty getting my vision from inside my head into a designer's head. With 99designs.com you're basically able to brain dump all your ideas and then 30-60 independent designers will submit a design and the winner will get paid however much you set the price to be. This gets you many different concepts for what your logo COULD look like to help you refine for yourself what you're actually looking for. You can set up similar contests for marketing materials and even websites too. All of this can cost a fraction of the price of a marketing agency where you only get one or two creative people looking at it.

Avoiding Tech Traps

Whatever you do, just make sure everything is backed up (the data, not the plumbing), should anything go wrong with a site. Yes, a good webmaster can even back up your entire site by creating a "mirror" site. We can't emphasize enough to beware of the many internet scams that come across your screen every day. For example, the phishing scams that look like they come from legitimate vendors (such as your bank). Read the return email address carefully. If it's one character off, that's the give-away. It's probably a fake. Contact the institution or company directly if in doubt. By all means, don't click on the link in the email. These unscrupulous operators want access to your data. Worse yet are the hijackers that will hold your computer hostage unless you pay them—known as "ransomware." Then there are the offshore tech support calls that claim they will fix all of your computer problems for a small fee. Allowing them access will end up costing you dearly.

All fears aside, the bottom line is that the barriers to entry for startup and early stage businesses have been lowered. So much legitimate technology that you can use affordably is at our fingertips without traditional cost and operations issues, so grab a hold of it and take a ride! (It will make you look really smart.)

Chapter X

What's Your System?

"Simple, Clear Purpose and Principles Give Rise to Complex and Intelligent Behavior. Complex Rules and Regulations Give Rise to Simple and Stupid Behavior."

—Dee Hock

Developing and Enforcing (Smart) Systems

Every day around 1000 companies go out of business. The number one reason businesses fail is because they lack structure and systems. Without processes and procedures businesses become disorganized and ineffective. Now, when most small businesses first start they don't really know what they're doing. It's trial by fire. I know when we started we were pretty clueless. I remember in my first month of business, it was a joy just to hear the phone ring. During one of the first calls, a potential client asked us to take a look at a pile of concrete that he had. You will recall the story from an earlier chapter, how we underestimated our expenses and lost money on the job. That "small" pile was really more like a backyard packed full of 80 pound slabs of concrete.

Being as desperate as we were at the time we simply gave in and accepted what he was willing to pay us. Big mistake. Big (stupid) mistake.

"Any Time We Have An Issue We Create a Policy to Prevent it Happening in the Future"

However, this was our first lesson in the value of systemizing. We now have a procedure for estimating properly by asking all the right questions to know almost exactly what our costs and profit margin will be. This example is just one of many different scenarios. We document everything. Any time we have an issue or hit a snag we write it down it in our Standard Operating Procedure (SOP) and put a policy in place to prevent it from happening in the future. I can then take that book and place it in the hands of someone brand new to the business and they will have little problem avoiding the mistakes we initially made. In short, you need to "manage the systems, not the people." It's important to keep in mind though, that the key to managing those systems is enforcement. If you don't enforce the systems then they're really just suggestions, and employees (as many of you know!) rarely follow suggestions (even if they're smart).

"Businesses that Incorporate Processes and Structures Accumulate Intrinsic Value"

The great thing about implementing procedures and policies is the structure they create. The more structure in your business, the better everything stays up and holds together and the less of YOU that is required to be there every day to DO every little thing. Businesses that incorporate processes and structures accumulate intrinsic value. These businesses allow their owners to step away from the day to day and focus more on their long-term personal vision. Personally, our long term vision is franchising Junk-A-Haulics® in every major US city, and by implementing a scalable structure it will enable us to easily replicate our successes in those new locations. Therefore, when making decisions we always return back to the central question of "can this be replicated in future operations?" So whether you want to scale up, as we do, or simply have a smoother running, more profitable current operation, building systems is the best (smartest) way to achieve your personal vision.

Before starting the business did I have any exposure to systems? Had I developed any systems before this? The answer? Very little. My first exposure to systems involved the sales process—prospecting, presenting, closing and asking for referrals, which I learned from my time selling knives at Cutco cutlery. When I graduated college and got a job in financial services, I refined my referral process, learning how to: ask for referrals, to qualify, as follows – 1. Get the affirmative – were you happy with the service? 2. Would you recommend it to others? 3. Then, to pull out a list of some Linkedin contacts of theirs that I might want to meet 4. Ask who they would feel comfortable making the intro to—or simply who they <u>don't</u> want me to call, which wound up getting me even more options.

In just three short years, we developed many systems that we use on a daily basis—for bookkeeping, collections, Accounts Receivable; for hauling, disposal/recyling; for donating, estimating, scheduling. And our HR functions, including recruiting, incentives, training/development; plus, our warehouse procedures, truck procedures, daily money envelopes, task management, phone/scripts, communication and internal safety procedures. So, you ask, how did I develop them? No secret—mostly by trial and error (sorry to disappoint you; I don't claim to be *that* smart). However, I learned a lot from reading, particularly the *E-Myth* by Michael Gerber, the seminal book on system creation. If you haven't read it, it's key to your success. I also learned from a peer advisory group. We'll share some of our "secret sauce" with you here.

You may be wondering, of all the systems above, how much did we develop ahead of time and how much was on the fly? Here's the reality: the basic systems were devised beforehand, but true time tested formalized ones were made after the fact....and often from some hard lessons learned. Take truck maintenance, for example. We had a truck that ran through oil very fast, but we didn't think too much of it. Then we found out later that it needed a whole new engine costing around $10,000—and all that could have been avoided if we had a maintenance process that would have caught the error early on. That process would have had us take it to the mechanic and do regular check-ups to key an eye on it, and another part of the system to more carefully monitor the oil levels of all our trucks. Double OUCH! Out of this experience now we developed a system to record oil levels on a weekly basis, on a daily basis note if the drivers found anything wrong with the truck before even going into it. Before this, a lot of times guys would notice stuff but forget to tell us. Now they have to record it before they even turn the key. (Brilliant, eh?)

Over time, we developed some fairly elaborate HR Systems for a small company. But it didn't start out that way. My first hire knocked on my door and said, "I need a job." At first I told him, "Sorry, I'm only a month in business and can't really afford anyone", and he said, "Whatever", and I said, "Whatever," and we just hired him. No testing, no vetting, nothing. (Lucky he wasn't an axe murderer.) And then 9 months later we hired 4 other people and they just talked to me for 20 minutes, or someone else said that they could be good and I replied, "Okay, you got the job." That's it; and as for training—I just said – "Ask the other guys! They'll show you". And that was it. So, you ask, "How'd that work out?" Not good.

After some high turnover, I realized that there needed to be some better systems in place to recruit and develop the talent (or in this case the muscle!) So, we developed our system, and it goes like this:

i.   1st step– Put out an ad, reach out to my whole network and get candidates in.

ii. 2nd step– Initial phone screening for essential qualities and job requirements.

iii. 3rd step– Open tryouts—come to the warehouse; see how they load a truck and work with other people and ask for directions and also do a mini 1 to 1 interview with everyone then.

iv. 4th step– Call back for formal interview an hour long—really get into the details.

v.   5th step– Trial period – 2-4 weeks paid work; evaluate with the guys.

vi. 6th step– Make it through everything else; then get the offer.

vii. 7th step - In depth training first to be a wing man and eventually to be a captain.

The point of all this is that our turnover was cut dramatically and the quality of our workers doubled. This resulted in more productivity and we became able to handle more jobs and even more satisfied customers.

Truck Logs: Making the Most of Every Job

Truck logs are a daily record that our haulers fill out to document the details of the day, as well as calculating how efficient they were. Our basic formula is to add up the total revenue for the day and then subtract the expenses, including employee hours (including insurance and taxes on employees), dumping expenses and fuel costs. And then based on that, the team leaders can calculate a "team cost" percentage. They get a performance bonus if this cost is low. It encourages the haulers to not waste time on the clock, to find ways to minimize dumping cost by recycling and donating more. It can be very tempting to just press a button and dispose of all the contents, but putting this process in place shows the workers directly the effects of their actions on our costs—and it encourages more recycling and donation, which we are committed to as a company. And with the fuel, they make sure the truck doesn't idle too much and they don't drive too fast or take any inefficient (stupid) routes. If the team cost is below our minimum target for operational efficiency then we give THEM the profits without costing the business anymore. We can do this because instead of paying the disposal places and the gas stations, we can pay the haulers with that money instead. And if they get the day's workload done fast, then they can get paid more money in less time. Everyone wins. Furthermore, it empowers the employees. It's a new type of entrepreneurship. The employees run the truck like their own mini-business, responsible for the profits and the losses. They really see the impact that they have on the company; they can view their work more objectively and think of it more like a business owner. (Way beyond stupid.) Let's give you a little scenario.

Suppose a haul brings in $1,000 in Gross revenue. Expenses are normally around $12/hour (we add $3 extra to get to the $15 because of workers comp and taxes) (Labor 6 hours @ $15 X 2 workers= $180) + gas $30 + dump $70 = total expenses of $280, so the team cost would be 28%. If the company's goal is 35% in expenses, for example, and the team achieves 28%, then they keep the 7% profit on top of their salary. It's also essential that we make sure we get paid the full amount so that the revenue remains high. For example, we charge extra for TVs and certain hazardous materials or paint cans where we have to buy cat litter to dry them out—which takes more man hours, so we need to charge more for this. It can be tempting to not want to have to explain all that to the customer and let it slide, but that's hurting the company so it has to be factored in. And then there is also upselling in general.

Consider how this cost accounting system might apply to your industry. For example, if you are engaged in craft manufacturing – making hand bags or decorative items. Perhaps landscaping – mulching – you might reduce supply costs, drive more efficiently and get the job done faster. The same might apply to construction, remodeling or paving, carpet installation or cabinetry. If you are in the cleaning business, getting the job done fast and upselling when a customer didn't mention dishes over the phone, but now all of a sudden they want it done – charge for that and you can lower the expenses by getting it done faster (providing you maintain the quality.)

See if you can apply our (very smart) formula to your business:

Daily Gross Revenue (For each individual team) – Direct Expenses (Cost Of Goods Sold) X the percentage.

So, what do we all live and die by in business? Collecting the money. For our commercial accounts, when we first started it was really bad – if someone hadn't paid me I would just put a note in my to do list, and half the time it might even get buried.(Definitely not smart.) Soon after that I made a basic accounts receivable spreadsheet and kept tabs on it that way. While this was an improvement, there was still no system in place to actually collect the money. It only made me aware of what was outstanding. Then I developed a process. We work on net 30 terms so the first step is as soon as it hits 30 days, we send a friendly reminder email forwarding the original invoice and following up to see if they received it. There are plenty of times when people simply either didn't see it amongst the millions of emails or they just plain forgot to take care of it.

"A Sale's Not a Sale Until The Money's in the Bank"

Many times this gets the payment in. Doing that alone cut our collection time in half. However, the next step would be for anyone who didn't respond to that initial email. We would start calling until we reached them and then get an agreement to send payment. That further cut down on any delays. However, for those few who were actively trying to delay the payment, we would have another reminder 15 days later referencing the last time we spoke and the fact that they need to pay. Finally, the last step in the process would be to have our attorney send out a letter requesting payment and by that point EVERYONE paid. This process made sure that we were paid for all the hard work we did and greatly improved our cash flow. As they say, "It's not a sale until the money is in the bank." So, did the money get into the bank? Yes. Of course! Now it did.

Enforcing Systems to Realize Your Vision

In addition to invoicing our commercial clients, we also needed to create a money collection system for all the cash and personal checks our haulers would collect on their jobs. How it used to work is, the guys would just do the job and then slap on the table whatever money or checks they had in their pockets from the past few days. This was a terrible (stupid) way to do things. First, there was the issue of cash. We had no idea whose cash job it came from or what the total sale was and if any of it was missing. Checks would often be crumpled. And if we did have to invoice, I was always running around trying to figure out WHO we had to invoice.

We remedied this by what I called the Envelope Collection System. We now require daily filling out of an envelope that had a pre-printed list prompting them to fill out the information of the exact jobs from that specific day, with the exact sale amount and the method of payment, and then the employees are required to deposit it into a lock box at the end of the day. They also sign and date the evelope. While this system did greatly improve the quality of our money collection, there were still loopholes. For example, on a day with all credit cards or invoices, they sometimes forgot to fill out an envelope, since technically there was no cash or check to put in it. Not submitting an envelope threw off the system because the office had no idea why that income was not there and would have to hunt it down.

This scenario illustrates why the enforcement is so important. In order to make sure we stuck to our process religiously, I had my Business Manager collect the envelopes daily so he would know right away if one was missing. If it was, then the haulers would have to spend their time explaining to the boss what happened, which no one wanted to waste their time doing. That quickly corrected the problem. If it

STILL happened, we would go the disciplinary route. The great thing was that this effective enforcement system rarely led to that. They almost always got with the program. Problem solved.

Then there was the problem of keeping our truck cabs clean. In order to do so, we came up with a simple process. On our daily truck logs, we had our crews check off that they emptied out the cab and then turn in the paper. That should have been enough, but without any enforcement it wasn't really anything. At one point, the cabs got so messy that it was like a movie scene with stuff dropping out left and right when we opened the doors. This was NOT the professional image we were going for. We then created an enforcement system whereby there would be 3 levels of inceasing consequences for not cleaning the cabs, and random checks to make sure that they were emptied. We posted this procedure on a highly visible flyer that would be seen multiple times every day to help reduce the "reminders" necessary on our part. Then we came up with a basic schedule to do the truck walk - throughs without having to remind ourselves to keep on top of it. This was less work for everyone and ensured that with little effort we would have sparkling clean cabs and happy employees. It is also a key example of "managing the systems and not the people."

Measure Everything

Measure everything. Set KPIs, or your Key Performance Indicators, and track the key metrics for what a growing and heathy company should look like. Some of the key indictors are: your business's gross revenue; net revenue; job profitability overall for the month, quarter and year, marketing sources (create a pie chart at the end of each month showing where the jobs came from). Also track your personal KPIs; the amount of referrals you get per month, the amount of referrals you GIVE OUT, the number of phone calls you want to make and your closing ratio for estimates that you give out—or whatever other trackable metrics that are relevant to your position and your industry. The more you can put a percentage on your personal and company's performance, you can then set out to objectively improve and enhance it. And you always have something to look at and see if you're moving the needle forward. Without the data you're just taking shots in the dark. (That would be stupid, wouldn't it?)

Chapter XI

Revving Your Engine; Sales

"A Person's Success in Life Can Usually be Measured by the Number of Uncomfortable Conversations He is Willing to Have."

—*Tim Ferriss*

Sell, sell, sell...
The Way We Were

I started selling door to door with wrapping paper at age 7. There was a bunch of crummy prizes, but at the very top they offered a telescope, which I thought was pretty much the coolest thing ever—so I had the motivation to hit the pavement and start hawking my wares at the ripe old age of 7. One of the interesting things I found was that surprisingly people were pretty receptive to it. I didn't have much guidance; I just went for it, winged it and learned on the fly that you just have to jump into things. Getting a basic plan initially is all you need. A lot of time we use planning and "strategy" as an excuse to delay action. After the sales are coming in then there's always time to refine and hone your craft.

The second biggest lesson I learned about sales–you NEED to tap into people's motivation and really get their interest. For my next foray into sales, in middle school I sold that great American staple, good old lemonade. I strategically picked the 4th of July, found a spot just two blocks from the entrance to one of the biggest fireworks displays in the county and plopped the stand where everyone had to walk by and see us. My motivation in this case was just to have fun and make some money. Well, at one point I went a little overboard and stood directly on the sidewalk, blocking traffic to sell my lemonade, but my family didn't really like that. I learned you can't be overly aggressive. Pigs get fat; hogs get slaughtered, as they say.

From this earth shattering, ground breaking experience, the take away— it's all about location and timing. Kids sell lemonade all day long and barely make anything before they quit after 2 hours and call it a day. But, in this case our location was so good that we were taking in close to what a professional adult vendor might make. Luckily we didn't have to get permits as middle schoolers! The other big lesson here; go where the need is—it's a hot night, people are thirsty and I filled their need. Also, we were the only ones there because a lot of people probably saw all the commotion and wouldn't want to deal with that. But that was really an opportunity to take in the most amount of business because we had the market cornered! Yeah baby!

"Asking Great Questions and Using those Questions to Identify Pain Points is the Foundation of Sales"

For me, high school was all focused on academics, but in college, I started to sell Cutco knives. First, you gotta know when to spot a good opportunity. My dad gave me a flyer for Cutco; at first I said, "No way, I ain't doing that. I already have a job as a bus boy at Macaroni Grill", but he insisted that I go. After getting the job on the spot, I called the restaurant before even leaving the Cutco office to quit working there, and start full time as a summer knife salesman...sharpening my skills! Here's what surfaced in learning that business. Asking great questions and using those questions to identify pain points is the foundation of sales. We had a $2,000 kit of knives but I wouldn't just start right off the bat pitching that. Instead, I would go through each and every knife and discuss how people in general could use it, but then I turned the question around and asked them specifically how *they* would use it. If they really had no idea or genuinely didn't seem to care, then I would mostly gloss over it. But the prospects that explained how they could use it—I really focused on those. Then, at the end of the sale I would go back and make a recommendation based on their feedback and they would magically think that I somehow put together the perfect combination of knives for them. But it was really just a matter of asking great questions to identify the pain and listening even better. If they later said that they wouldn't use a particular knife that they originally said they could use, I would simply go back and repeat their own words to them. Asking great questions is the single most important thing I learned there.

So where do you find customers? With prospecting, your warm market is the best way to go – your family, your friends and more importantly, everyone *they* know. When I first had to call these people I experienced extreme anxiety about doing so, for fear of sounding stupid or any other type of head trash that might come along. However, my managers at the time said just call one person and then see how you feel. I was able to overcome the anxiety because having to call just one person was a much easier task then staring down a list of 50 names. After calling that one person, I challenged myself to call just one more. Because the first one didn't bite my head off, I was able to keep making progress one by one. It was still tough at times, but equipped with this method made it infintely easier. As you no doubt have heard, referrals make prospecting much easier. You should always ask for them. It's the toughest part of the sale because you are already asking people for their time and money, but if you get the affirmative that they were happy with the service, then you need to get it in your head that it's just someone else who you can help and make another happy customer. Always, always ask. That's how you keep your sales engine flowing.

Everyone needs support. Sales is a tough gig emotionally, so having a big support team is essential. I never would have sold what I did without it. Now, you won't always have warm, qualified referrals and leads. Sometimes ya just gotta take the plunge and make those cold calls. Still, there are ways to warm up the cold call. Here's what I did. I got my high school directory and called everyone in the book, whether I knew them or not, but I tried to find some kind of connection to warm up the call. Even the simplest things can be used to get an "in" and separate you from the countless other people vying for your potential customers' attention—not to mention his or her dollars.

After college, I learned about sales from a different angle when I got a job in financial services. Working in financial services was a big 180 degree turn from meeting with housewives on a summer sunny day as a college kid. Gone were the days of instant closes after talking for 40 minutes about vacation plans and cooking habits. Unlike my Cutco experience, where my young age helped, now my age was seen as somewhat of a hindrance because people aren't exactly bursting at the seems trying to hand a 21 year-old kid their entire life savings to manage. This is where I learned the value of persistence, patience and relentless follow up to a major degree. Just to get one appointment would usually take 100 phone calls (unless I was able to get a warm lead), but also being young my network was tiny so I had to work from the ground up. That is where true persistence comes into play with relentless follow up – always agreeing when to follow up and never missing a chance to do so. As long as you're not a pest, this is essential.

"The Biggest Secret of Sales, Beyond the Nice Smile and the Good Handshake, is Simply Being Organized."

The biggest hidden secret of sales, beyond the nice smile and the good handshake, is simply being organized. Knowing who you have to call and when, and having great notes, allows you to always be on top of that process. The follow up becomes automatic; I would just check my well maintained call list for the day and wouldn't have to worry about anything else, or worry about something slipping through the cracks. I say hidden secret because organizational skills are rarely the first thing talked about for being a successful sales person, but it is absolutely critical to one's success.

So, as a young person trying to gain the trust of mostly older prospects, I had to make it very clear that I was there to solve a problem. Most importantly, I had to separate myself from the pack. Before doing anything, I would never talk about features and benefits, or about how great and fantastic we are—not even how happy they will be working with us. Instead, I focused on a purely fact finding process— learning not only about their professional objectives and financial picture, but even the prospects' personal goals, because that would allow us to make a truly comprehensive set of recommendations.

Almost all of my first meetings would be spent listening to them speak, and I would just think of ways to help them meet their objectives. This builds great credibility and trust, and lowers resistance so we don't waste time doing the dance of them being sold to. In addition, it was all about getting the EARLY NO—being upfront and telling them that either one of us can walk away at any point for whatever reason if it's clear that we might not be a good fit – once again preventing anyone from wasting their time. This technique is also called the "upfront contract"—a highly useful sales technique taught in Sandler® Sales Training. It's important to acknowledge objections before you can overcome them – I gave the prospect the opportunity to raise objections; this made them feel comfortable having an honest conversation with me. And then, of course I did my best to overcome the objections—BUT, if it's a truly good objection I wouldn't just dismiss it out of hand. I would take it under serious consideration, and if it revealed that the service was not a good fit at this time I would let them know that. Lastly, I did what said I was going to do. So simple, but it rarely happens – people remember what you say even if you say it off handedly. People take it as your word, so even minor things that you may have said you must follow through on. And this reinforces your integrity, commitment and credibility to your prospect.

Networking Like a Madman; Back-Filling Your Pipeline

When I first started Junk-A-Haulics, I began the process in a similar fashion to how I found people in my financial serices gig. I would make a list of a bunch of companies and just start calling them. It felt good going through a lot of contacts quickly, and I got to speak with a lot of people, but no one knew who I was and they had no reason to do business with me as a random voice on the phone. For example, recently I was in a meeting and someone walks in, interrupts us and gives me a flyer. As soon as she had left, that flyer was already being shredded into a million pieces. Why? Because we are innundated with people trying to contact us, and with so many choices we want to know the company and the person's background before we consider doing business with them. That's why referrals are so powerful. They are implied endorsements of someone's quality and credibility. AND we're in the junk removal business, so why would we want more junk!

At some point I was invited to an event at my county level Chamber of Commerce. I always knew networking was a great avenue to develop business, but I never thought that it could be nearly your entire sales stratagy. When I first went to an event called Business Connections, I still had some trepidation. I didn't feel very comfortable in this room of 200 people, many of whom seemed to know each other already. It was very overwhelming, in a sea of suits and heels. However, I decided to fully commit myself to regularly going to meetings (don't worry; no one converted me—this wasn't a cult!) and also doing a number of one-to-one meetings. I was also fortunate to have several of the more experienced networkers make some initial introductions and give me some tips.

By committing to networking in this group as a full-time objective, I was able over the next 6 months, to go from zero referrals to an average monthly pull of 8-10 referrals and 6-7 closed pieces of business—and it has only gone up from there. Now, a number of years in and a whole lot of jobs completed, and I can say networking is the cornerstone of our growth.

There are 4 main commandments of networking that I utiltize to very effective ends. No praying necessary; just follow 'em!

1. Find Strategic Centers of Influence & Connectors

CENTERS OF INFLUENCE: Someone who regularly comes across people who can use our service and therefore can put us in touch with them.

CONNECTOR: Someone who is not necessarily related to our business at all, but knows how to bring people together for their mutual benefit.

At one point, I realized that if I had 20 contacts who referred me just 1 lead a month I could make an entire business with just 20 people. Centers of Influence are basically your sales force. You can go out and shake all the hands you want but you're still just one person. If you build an army of strategic alliances then you will never have to worry about getting business in again. (Very smart indeed.)

I maintain a hyper focus on networking strategically by joining groups where my key centers of influence hang out. Like all marketing, you have to be targeted. And when I go to these events I always go in with a clear goal. I want to get at least 2-4 one-to-one meetings with a potential strategic center of influence. I divide the people in the room into five categories based on their business and/or referral potential. I usually write the number directly on someone's business card when I receive it. A 5 is a contact who is highly targeted and relevant to my business and I think there could be a lot of value shared both ways. A 4 contact is also someone who I think has good potential to either do business with or cross refer each other but needs to be qualified a little further. A 3 is someone who may not necessarily be in a very relevant industry but is a strong connector. In order to identify what a good connector looks like, I usually can pick them out at networking events because they are the ones who are always gregarious, interactive with the other attendees, or simply smiling and joking around with people. If they are doing any of those things then there's a good chance they are experienced networkers who know a lot of people (aka they have a deep Rolodex). I find that the 3s (as I defined them) are often times an underrated category but they should not be dismissed! Then we come to the 1s and the 2s. These people have no relevance to my industry, do not appear to be as engaged with others and in general, simply don't give any indication that a fruitful relationship would develop with them. I am, of course always very friendly and chat with people in this category (you never know where business may come from!), but there simply isn't enough time in the day to meet with everyone, so I just meet with 5s, 4s and 3s. Just like with your task list, you have to prioritize who you spend your time with—including how you spend your time following up with people as well. If I reach out to a 3 level contact but they don't seem terribly receptive, then I don't waste time banging on their door. However, if it's a 5 level contact I am way more persistent (although never a pest!). By using this model of prioritizing your contacts you will have a much more results driven model of networking.

"Meeting 10 People 10 Times Will Prove More Valuable Than Meeting 100 People 1 Time"

2. Commit More Time to a Few Groups.

Meeting 10 people 10 times will prove more valuable than meeting 100 people 1 time. At one point, I visited 17 different BNI chapter meetings in one month, all of which met at 7AM. I was networking like a madman, and even though it was efficient, it wasn't effective. *Networking is farming, not hunting.* Relationships are like crops to be cultivated, not animals to be slain. Now, I would rather see the same 10 people 10 times than 100 people 1 time. It's all about creating powerful strategic partnerships where you regularly help each other's businesses succeed. If you spread yourself too thin then you get lost in the shuffle.

You have to stay on people's radar. People forget you very easily. You have to stay top of mind, and regular touches deepen the relationship. Consistency: pick one event and never miss it. Become a household name in that particular networking event. The chamber I belong to that holds 10 events per month. However, I usually go to only 1 or 2, and despite that I'm one of the top people being referred because I NEVER miss those particular meetings or any of the follow up one-to-one meetings.

3. Nothing Happens at Networking Events

You may remember this scene where you go in, shake a lot of hands and nothing comes of it. In the moment when you meet a new person you're excited to see them and get to know them better. Later on you're confused when nothing happens. The reality is that almost nothing happens the first time you meet someone at a networking event. It's like a first date! No one gets married on the first date. (Unless this is Vegas) The magic happens AFTER the event. When you get a chance to do face to face, one-to-one meetings you can do a deep dive and find the treasure. Get to know about the other person's interests and even get to know them as a person. This is a lot of work and takes a lot of time, but setting up those meetings is what builds the connections that will actually make networking work. When you go to the events, you're really just there to find more people to get the opportunity to get to know, and reinforcing your relationship with people you already met with. Simply put, networking is just about making friends.

4. Give as Much as Possible, and you Will Get Back Ten-Fold

This last point is by far and away the most important one. There is hardly anything that people hate more than being pitched (accept maybe death—or maybe root canal). The act of giving unselfishly has an inverse effect because it creates a feeling of reciprocity whereby the other person feels the need to give back. It is one of the most satisfying feelings, being able to connect two people without expecting anything and seeing them better off than where they were before. You can do this any number of ways. The weakest way is to just give someone a name and a number and give them permission to use your name. It's okay but it's not quite as powerful. A second, more powerful way is to make the introduction yourself, either by speaking with them over the phone or an email introduction where you directly and strongly endorse and recommend this person you want to help. The ultimate way to make an introduction is to bring the two people together in person and personally introduce them while you're there. It paves the way to make a truly meaningful connection and bypass any of the hesitation any parties may have, plus you get to reconnect with your contact as well.

The first type of introduction I do not recommend—as it basically says you can tolerate helping but you don't really want to go out of your way at all. The second type I find to be ideal for the majority of connections, simply because there is only so much time in a day, so you do have to be realistic with your schedule. The third type of introduction should be used for any strategic relationship that you want to put in the forefront of your networking plan.

Every holiday season I go through the list of business partners to give gifts to and I categorize the people into 3 tiers: business friend, a connection that gave 1-3 referrals and power partners—the people really feeding my business with qualified leads. I am continually amazed by how many people are added each year to our multi-referral partners list and our power partner list. Many of these people were mere strangers the previous year and are now one of hundreds of people who fill our pipleline with jobs to complete.

Much of that started with me thinking of them first and asking a very simple question: "How Can I Help You?" That is one of the most important questions in business—and hands down, the number 1 question to be a networking pro.

Sales Masters: Advice from the Experts

Al Turrisi – President, Turrisi & Associates

Let's get the view from 50,000 feet. We asked career sales managers and trainers for their best advice. Al breaks it down to these four critical areas you need to control.

1. **The Model- Identify Your Ideal Prospect.** Ask these questions: where do your prospects live or work? If you sell business to business, what are the industry types? Who is the decision maker? What types of problems do the people have? What solutions do you as a salesperson bring to solve their problems?
2. **Sales Process**- You need to establish how you get the first appointment, what to do on the first appointment and how to qualify the opportunity.
3. **Pipeline**- Your prospects fall into categories, including cold, suspect, warm and hot, according to their sales potential. The sales process measures the quality and the quantity of the sales pipeline.
4. **Sales person's ability to manage the pipeline**- It's a science. The salesperson needs a strong desire to succeed, even when it becomes difficult.

If you just started, what's most critical for you? Remaining positive and so committed nothing can stop you. It's best to seek out and learn from an expert. So, we asked our expert What are some of the biggest myths surrounding sales? His response? "Everyone's a prospect." Maybe for someone, but not necessarily for you. "The most outgoing person makes the best sales person." Not always true.

We asked Al for his favorite closing tips. Well, surprise, surprise. He didn't offer any. Why? Because, according to Al, it's not closing; it's a matter of the prospect buying. It's a question of whether you really understand their issues and offered the best solutions. If so, then they'll want to buy. The key is great qualification or disqualification.

You can find more about Al Turrisi at: www.turrisiassociates.com

Chapter XII

Marketing: Be Visible; Get Noticed; Be Remembered

"If at First the Idea is Not Absurd, Then There Will be No Hope For It."

—*Albert Einstein*

It's not Just Visibility; It's Being Disruptive and Noticeable

In one of my first meetings with my busienss advisor Chris Lipper, he told me I should be in our local Saint Patrick's Day Parade. Before I even got a chance to respond he was already typing away an introduction to someone he knew who might be able to help me get in. So I made sure I did everything possible to get into the parade that year, and I was thrilled when I was accepted. Finally, on the morning of the parade, I jumped out of bed with anticipation and my phone rang. It was one of my employees saying, "Jeff, it's 35 degrees out, pouring rain, no one is going to be in attendance, and none of us want to stand outside getting drenched and shivering for

5 hours." I was devastated, but I rallied the rest of the team and guaranteed them that we were going to make this work **and** have a great time!

So I went out and bought the craziest Saint Patrick's Day stuff I could find, like giant green hats and oversized shamrock sunglasses, 'Kiss Me I'm Irish' ties and then we put mattresses in the back of our dump truck to stand on. We put the super springy ones on the top of the pile, which turned our truck into the world's craziest bouncy fort, and that morning we all had a blast. This became one of our most memorable and enjoyable marketing maneuvers to date. But it wasn't just about being visible, it was about being disruptive and noticeable. There were plenty of other businesses in the parade with a truck simply going down the line, but we really turned heads. We were arguably one of, if not the most, attention-grabbing group at the event—and that's saying a lot for an Irish parade. It not only increased business but enhanced our profile, showed our company's personality and raised our brand awareness.

In my second year in business, I decided that I was going to sponsor an event and give a presentation in front of 200 people—without any previous public speaking experience. I was slightly terrified, but the one thing I knew I had to do was make a big splash to get people's attention. At one point I thought up the idea of bringing a giant refrigerator into the banquet hall where the event was being held. I thought how ridiculous would that be if we plopped an old, dirty refrigerator right down in the middle of such a high end and upscale venue. Then at some point I thought, hah I'm totally gonna do that. And while we're at it, how about we litter the long corridors on the way to the main ballroom with a bunch of old junky furniture and stick our Junk-A-Haulics signs on them to really drive the point home? Needless to say, we created exactly the kind of splash we were looking for. WHY? Because it was different; it was disruptive. People noticed and people remembered Junk-A-Haulics. As a result, it basically doubled the business we were doing with my chamber members.

The "B" Word: Branding - Be A Category of one

How do you create a successful brand? Well, thank you for asking. Start by defining what you can be exceptional at. Be a "category of one"—don't compete with others; compete in your own space. When we first got our new truck we couldn't afford to wrap it with graphics. The funds just weren't there yet, so we were kind of stuck. After a few months went by, we were on a job and a lady said to us, "Oh, I thought you were a professional company." My heart sank...that was pretty much the absolute worst thing we could have heard. Everything we were doing was designed to exude professionalism, and yet this very off the cuff honest comment threw me for a loop. We learned that as well as creating the experience of the brand, you also need to have the appearance of the brand. You have to live the brand in all ways at all times. You even have to brand yourself personally. I did this by replacing my last name in introductions with Junk-A-Haulics so I became known as "Jeff Junk-A-Haulics." You need to condition people to identify your company and yourself. You want to become synonymous with your product or service in the consumer's mind, as well as easy to remember. It's the same reason why I don't tell people some of the other services that we do when I first meet them because I want the brand to be NARROW. I want it to be very clear and not confusing whatsoever.

So, let's define our terms here. Whiteboard, please...It's important not to confuse your *brand* with your *brand indicia*. Simply put, your logo, your color scheme, your font (typeface) are your brand indicia – they are indicators of your brand, but not the brand itself. Your BRAND is a specific set of expectations of performance that are associated with your product or service. For example, cleanliness, professionalism, clean cut, fast, friendly, etc – THAT'S our brand promise.

Meanwhile, back to the indicia...When picking colors, do your research on what emotions various colors evoke. For example, blue is a calming color – that's why we picked it. Yellow is psychologically the happiest color. (Why do you think Van Gogh used it so much—or was it Gaugin?) Red is alarming, but exciting. Green symbolizes health and growth (yeah, that's probably why Green Giant chose it). Now, how hard do you wanna hit 'em? Get this: the single highest impact color combination is black and yellow; the second highest is red with white lettering – this is based on studies from the signage and outdoor advertising (billboard) industry.

So, after picking your color, you need to pick the right font to communicate your brand. First, you need an easily readable font in any size. If it's tough to read (that would

117

be stupid), how are you going to be memorable? The font signifies the feeling you want to evoke. Ours is fun and playful and the font represents that to tell people the feeling we're trying to convey. Other fonts might be more serious if it's for a law firm, or an edgy font for a design studio, or a bold font for a motivational speaker. You get the idea.

However you design your brand indicia, it should be translatable across various media platforms so it plays well on your shirt, on a billboard, on a vehicle and on your website. If it doesn't work in any of those formats, then rework it. Don't get hung up on overly artistic designs; make something that's simple, clear and memorable.

As we mentioned before, based on the title of Joe Calloway's book, you want to aspire to become a "Category of One." Don't compete with others; compete in your own space. Often times we look at other successful companies and try to emulate them, thinking that's what we need to be doing. "Hey, let's be big like they are. It worked for Google or Amazon, but if you do that then you'll always be playing in their game, which they're clearly better at!! Because it's THEIR GAME!!! We do some things differently. For example, rolling down a red carpet like the customer is a movie star. Why? It's red because, sure a painter can roll down a paint covered tarp—but that doesn't scream "professional." While it may be professionally minded, everyone else is doing that. It's all about taking it a step further, elevating it and making it permeate absolutely *everything*. EVERYONE says they're professional; that's not unique – it's all in the execution. I read about a newspaper and they said focus on putting names in the editorial. Ssomeone replied, "Okay, everyone does that; that's newspaper 101. No big deal." He replied, "NO. Our mantra is NAMES, NAMES, NAMES" – it's 10 times what other people are doing, and as a result, while other newspapers were crashing, people were jumping on it like crack to see if they had their little moment of fame, to the newspaper's huge benefit. OOOOH, is MY NAME or my family's name going to be in there? Play on the ego – but hey, it works![4]

The differentiator? It's a matter of *degree*. Wearing booties so you don't track everything in, for example. It's fine to to start with the basics of what made another company succesful. In our industry it was having clean cut, uniformed, friendly, polite, well spoken haulers, but you need to go FURTHER than that. Another thing you need to do is to look for the FLAWS in your competition—especially the companies that are very good—because they all have them. For example, I noticed vehicle (appearance) maintenance was lacking. Even the big brands have rust on their trucks. As soon as it becomes noticable, we cut in half the time we allow rust to be on there, whereas other companies may let it go longer. Here's a simple, obvious one. We give a thank you gift at every job – whether it's a magnet, chocolate or some other goodies. It's all about that extra cherry on the top! For us, as a service business, a key aspect of professionalism is the call ahead. We give the customer an arrival time frame, emphasizing it multiple times. We say it 2-3 times per call to drill it in, and then we take it a step further. We not only call when we're on the way, we also call to let them know when

---

[4] *Made to Stick,* Chip and Dan Heath

within the arrival WINDOW we're going to actually arrive. So if it's a 2-4 PM estimated arrival, but we already know at 11:30AM that it's going to be closer to 3PM, we'll let them know so they can do their grocery shopping, etc. But wait— there's more! We take it yet another step FURTHER. We often call AFTERWARDS to ask how'd we do. Especially in this day and age they're not expecting a real person on the other end just calling to see if they're happy, and it gives us the opportunity to improve and get a review online from them, as well.

You must continue to enhance the experience. In our case, that means sweeping up after the job, which is common practice among the top companies, but if they need basic cleaning we can even do that—or refer it out to a trusted colleague if they need a more elaborate deep clean. But either way it's one more thing they can move off of their check list. When it comes to a real estate deal, timing can be critical for people that need to make a closing date, or to vacate. Helping them remove junk and clean up can sometimes mean the difference between successfully completing the transaction or not. Speaking of which, we also bring a trusted partners list. On any job, if the customer expresses frustration in any other area of their home care, we refer on the spot a trusted advisor— such as professional organizer, a carpet cleaner, a painter, etc. It's all about communicating that cohesive message and ensuring that your operations back it up.

Understanding that the essence of a BRAND = EXPERIENCE, ask yourself what's the EXPERIENCE of working with us? One of my all time favorite brand experiences is with Virgin Atlantic Airways. The first time I flew with them, right off the bat I noticed that the entire cabin interior was lined with beautiful and elegant mood lights. This was something that at the time I had never experienced on United® or Delta® even once. Furthermore, in my past experiences I'm used to a flight crew who is usually either slightly grumpy or at best moderately pleasant for the most part. When I boarded the Virgin Atlantic plane there was a welcoming party! I felt like a celebrity just climbing over to my seat in coach. They also offered a wide array of complimentary drinks and food. At the time, I was with a bunch of college students who took liberties with the libations. (What a surprise!) And by that I mean that there were constantly hands up for service. Yet, despite this, the ultra friendly (not to mention attractive!) staff members kept smiles on their faces and remained upbeat throughout the flight. THAT is the ultimate brand expereince. Some of these effects I'm sure cost more money, but as a result of this, not only did I want to come back immediately, but I also told everyone all the time about it. Those extra dollars invested by Virgin Atlantic paid off in spades. Personally, our goal is to become the Virgin Atlantic of the junk removal industry. (I may be crazy, but I'm not stupid!)

One of the biggest mistakes you can make when creating a brand is being too broad. You have to pick ONE thing to focus on and be the best at. For example, when we were discussing the key element of the "Junk-A-Haulics experience" we were debating among being the friendliest, the greenest and the most professional. At one point in the conversation, someone suggested "Hey, they're all excellent attributes; why not just focus on all three?" Wrong. It seems like a common sense statement, but then you have no differentiating factor. You can't be the best at three different brand identities, and if you try you'll just become a watered down version of those three things. It's a Jack-of-All-Trades and master of none situation. You are either one or none.

Keep in mind that the other brand qualities can still be a key part of your experience. They just can't be the primary one identified with you. You also have to look at the competitive landscape and see where you fit in. In our case, there was already another company who focused on being green, so it would make no sense to compete on their turf (get it, green?) when we can just invent our own. When you pick your brand identity you need to give people something big to talk about with everyone they know. You need to create an experience that was so great and unique that they are bursting at the seams just waiting to talk about it with people. These people will then become your brand ambassadors.

What About the Press?

Once again, let's define our terms here. Publicity, or public relations (PR), involves getting the media to tell your story. The job of PR is to raise your profile and credibility, and to create a climate favorable to sales. The job of advertising is to drive sustained traffic and sales. Hence, your PR should come first, and your advertising will have a greater ring of authenticity. The problem is that many businesses may not have newsworthy stories to tell. The media frowns on blatant self-promotion. However, a good publicist can find the story in your business that you may have overlooked. If you have an altruistic or charitable tie-in, for example, many media outlets will tell that story. The media like the unusual, quirky stories as well.

The Value of PR

Here's why I personally think PR is so valuable. When it comes to scaling up and fast growth, I find PR to be by far one of the top ways to achieve that. The reason is that PR instantly builds you a profile. It establishes you as credible –since it's a 3rd party source—it's not just your mom who loves you, it's the media. It's a quick way to separate yourself from the pack. If you have a company and there are 5 other people who do what you do, and you're all saying that you're great, but if the "New York Times" features you and says your great, now all of a sudden you're competing in a new league.

Perception dictates everything; we operate in a herd mentality— a "follow the leader" world. Everyone wants to know what's trending!!! Take this true story, for example. It comes right out of the social psychology literature. It's known as "The Ladies of Decatur" study. In Decatur, Illinois, the owner of a dress shop placed a dress prominently in the window. He ran a full-page ad in the local newspaper advertising the dress. The dress did not sell. The next week, the mayor's wife bought that dress and wore it to a ribbon-cutting ceremony. Her picture appeared on the front page of the same newspaper where the dress was previously advertised. The dress then sold repeatedly. It's all about influence.

Keep in mind that you need to have an ongoing PR campaign, not just a one-off story. While advertising is what you say about yourself and PR is what the media says about you, you don't have control over the message or the timing in PR. There's always an upside and a downside to everything in business and in life. Just remember that a PR campaign can include everything from press releases, to guest appearances and interviews, to special events. With the proliferation of online media, you can garner press by guest blogging, posting videos to YouTube and other social media channels. Nearly all traditional media outlets now have an online presence, so if you get press, it will likely end up on the internet. This helps you to increase your digital footprint, and therefore, makes you more searchable online. Most every press account that appears online will have your website, which results in more backlinks to your site.

"Brainstorm in Pictures." When coming up with an idea, one of the most effective ways I've found is "brainstorming in pictures." What this means is, you want to think of a story with a picture that can say it all. A story has legs if it can be easily summed up with a simple visual. When pitching to news organizations you can let the picture tell the story and the words will follow easily. Some of the story hooks we hung our own press releases on included the following topics: Donations to the Wounded Warrior Project, Donations to a Toy Drive and the young entrepreneur angle. Here's a few more approaches we took to seek out press coverage: Recycling/eco friendly hook, saving real estate transactions by removing last minute junk, hoarders, de-Cluttering/Organization, E-waste/data destruction, treasure finding—the crazy stuff we find and anything we do that is fun/unconventional. Look for the story behind the story.

The old saying goes, "If a dog bites a man, it's not news; but if a man bites a dog, it's news." So, go bite a dog if you want press coverage! Better yet, hire a freelance publicist or a PR firm. They already have connections to the media and can accelerate the process for you. We'll be watching.

The Scientific Entrepreneur: The Testing and Measuring Form of Marketing

When starting a business there is often the tempation to want to research things to death. Conventional wisdom says you should go in with a plan and then execute on that plan. This make sense. However, it's a fairly ineffective way to do things because as soon as your well thought out plan interacts with and encounters the real world (how things actually work), a lot of times that awesome plan gets totally scrapped or reworked completely. The best way to figure out your marketing (or other plans) is to quickly gather a list of theories about how and what you think will be effective marketing strategies and then put them to the test, as if it was a science experiment. Your ideas on what you think will work are the hypotheses and then you test them one by one through actions and compare the results. Sometimes, in spite of your best efforts, you end up engaging in trial by fire.

By making it an objective game to play it is far less overwhelming because you can simply test and measure, test and measure, test and measure. For example, when we began our junk removal business, we thought property managers would be a great group of people to target and network with. So we came up with a formula for the number of property managers we wanted to contact, how frequently we'd contact them, the follow up method after we reached them and then we recorded the number of jobs it brought in and in how much time. Then we would pick another market segment; for example, storage facilities. For that target, we would list the different metrics to track for approaching that group of people and then we could simply compare the results. It turned out that while some property managers did prove to be effective, we had three times as much success resulting from pursuing storage facilities. At that point you can create an ROI based on the amount of money spent pursuing both groups and the effectiveness for the time spent. By doing so in this case and any related ones, you're able to put a specific number and even a dollar amount to understand the effectiveness and tailor your time investment accordingly. It's all about working smarter, not harder. Anyone can go out and contact everyone on the planet; sure you'll get some people to buy, but the "spray and pray" method is a thing of the past. We have limited time and we have to maximize it. This is a far more strategic time saving and money maximizing approach.

You can also survey the potential target group ahead of time as well, to gauge their level of interest and see what the response is. It's not worth making a major effort on something that will yield only a tepid response. Everything can be tracked in a spreadsheet, and when viewed objectively in this form, it becomes a very precise operation. You don't have to worry about doing work that will lead to spinning your wheels. And it can prove fun to track the results, as well. Every test can also become its own little project and you can divide the projects amongst multiple people in your company to encourage ownership of their individual tests.. Ask your prospects what products or services they want, what they dislike about their current suppliers, what it would take to make them change to you—and even whether they have used a product or service like yours, why or why not? Market research has traditionally been the foundation of a sound marketing strategy. Today, we're simply reinventing how it's done.

Chapter XIII

Never Walk Alone

"Behind Every Great Leader, at the Base of Every Great Tale of Success, You Will Find an Indispensable Circle of Trusted Advisors, Mentors and Colleagues."

—*Keith Ferrazzi*

The Importance of Mentorship

When I sold wrapping paper at the incredibly mature age of seven, I at least had some parental guidance. When I sold knives for Cutco, I had guidance from my managers. And, when I sold financial services, I had the benefit of a great program with experienced people to guide me. With my own business, Junk-A-Haulics, if I had guidance even earlier in the game, we could have avoided more (stupid) mistakes. (Also known as expensive learning experiences.)

First, I filed my trademark way later then I should have. Even though I started using the name Junk-A-Haulics as early as 2009, I didn't file for trademark protection until 2014. In the interim, someone else filed a trademark for a similar name:

"JUNK A HAUL IT", which, while it's different, (and if you ask me, not nearly as good!!) the trademark office said it was too similar. They would not let me proceed without either getting permission from the other party to issue my mark or flat out buying their mark. This created a year and a half saga of delays, lawyer's fees and sleepless nights (not to mention all my marketing efforts were on hold for fear of not getting the Intellectual Property). Eventually, after hiring a great trademark attorney, we got it sorted out. But all of this could have been avoided if I had simply talked to an attorney much earlier (early is smart). Plenty of them will offer free initial consultations, so at least get the facts; then you can decide how you want to proceed.

For the most part, I was pretty good about seeking out help for the more obvious sales and operational aspects of running a business, but it's the issues that you might not think to get help for that will come back and bite you the most...and they did. The least interesting but most important is probably regulatory issues. When I started the business I had an inclination that we might need to get a license (even though it was a non-skilled trade), but at the time my initial partner didn't think too much of it. He said if we need to get it, then it will only take a week or two. After initially operating for a few months under the radar, we were told by the transfer station operators that a license was required. So, we had to completely shut down operations until we got one. We shrugged this off at first, thinking it was only a week or two's delay. Much to our great dismay, it took 3 hours digging online just to find the application (the name of the form was just letters and numbers—thank you for all your help, government!) Then, it got worse. Once we downloaded the app we ran out of ink just printing it because it was over 200 pages long. Not only that, but they even wanted social security numbers for both of our parents, for our siblings and for the people we lived with, so that they could do background checks on everyone we know. (I guess they wanted to make sure we weren't part of the cast of the Sopranos!)

And then it got even worse. After finally completing the application we asked how long it would take to get the license and we found out that it would take over a year and a half. Game over. At this point, hearing this news, my initial partner became my ex-partner, as he decided to let me buy him out of the business. I now had to carry on alone and put my life on hold for nearly the next 2 years when all was said and done. All of this could have been avoided if, instead of making assumptions (stupid), we had consulted people in the industry and people involved in the regulatory aspects to become fully educated on these matters (smarter).

When I started Junk-A-Haulics, I was on a tightrope without a net. I quickly realized that I needed labor help, but after the first few months it became apparent that I needed some business guidance as well. The light first went off to do this when I sat down with a facilitator for The Alternative Board (TAB), which is a peer advisory group of business owners (basically like a mastermind group). He asked me about my business and what areas I was looking to improve, or thought I could make major changes in. As I started to go down the list it became so long that he pretty much had nothing to sell me on. I knew I needed help. What appealed to me specifically about TAB was that I would get coaching not only from a business professional, but also from 8 other entrepreneurs who all had similar challenges and could each offer their unique insights (definitely smart). It's not like hiring a consultant who just comes in, tells you what to do and then leaves. Here you have ongoing, continuous access to the different business owners at a fixed, affordable cost. Individual executive coaching can help too, but a lot of those coaches charge upwards of $2,000+ a month, which can be pretty prohibitive for early stage businesses. When your business can afford the individual professional guidance, I do recommend that in addition to a peer advisory group.

Running a business requires a multitude of skills, but most of us only possess a limited number of those (even if we're not stupid). So, in order to fill those gaps, we need to seek out people in all different capacities. In addition to using the paid advisory services, you should put your tax dollars to work and look into other available options that are sponsored through the government (see, they're not all bad). Here are a few services to consider:

- Business incubators and accelerators: some are located at community colleges
- SCORE (Service Core of Retired Executives). Counselors all over who volunteer their time. You can access some good talent that way.
- US SBA. The Small Business Administration has management assistance—not just loans!
- SBDC's. Small Business Development Centers.

- University Professors. Some adjunct faculty are active business owners.

Additionally, through networking you should develop your own personal non-paid advisors, such as people in your industry who have tremendous experience with the issues you're facing. You can also tap into a trade association if your industry has one. Also, consider befriending retirees and later stage entrepreneurs who were already successful, as well as people who are around your level but maybe a few steps ahead and can offer really sound advice. Lastly, I pick EVERYONE'S brain (don't worry, I'm not a zombie). I did learn very early on from my father that you should gain as much information as possible from people who know stuff that you don't know and be a total sponge. I am continually operating on the belief that there is very little that I know compared to how much information is out there. When I studied Philosophy in college, one of my favorite quotes was, "The more I learn, the more I realize how little I know." I found this comment very fascinating because of just how true it is. When you don't know a subject very well you may assume that there are just a few things you need to learn about, because you're operating on the surface level. However, once you really dive into a topic, you learn just how vast it is. In all the different areas of business, you can always learn from people of all backgrounds and levels of experience because everyone has unique perspectives. Never worry about being rejected because most people will say yes to offering information and advice just for asking. People want to be helpful.

Chapter XIV

Learning is Lifelong; Educate Yourself

"There are Three Kinds of Men. The Ones That Learn by Readin'. The Few Who Learn by Observation. The Rest of Them Have to Pee on the Electric Fence for Themselves."

—*Will Rogers*

At one point in high school I started seeing the value of learning outside of what was assigned to me. I became interested in alternative history, which discussed historical events that were rarely mentioned in class text books, as well as a different depiction of events that were mentioned but could have arguably been spun in a different way. What intrigued me about these ideas is that they challenged the status quo and got me to think differently. The accuracy of the ideas is less important than the simple action of questioning everything. Being inquisitive forced me to evaluate everything on its own merit rather than based on what I was told to think about it. This aligned well with my entrepreneurial nature as an independent thinker.

When I went off to college I temporarily enrolled as an economics major, thinking that it was the most "practical" concentration, especially if I wanted to go into business in any form. However, as I took the classes I felt stifled by the lack of critical thought involved. I felt like I was just absorbing information. What I was really interested in was understanding the "why" behind the information. Shortly around that time I stumbled on a philosophy class. Being a typical college kid, I was frequently running late to class and the professor thought I was not interested—or just plain out of it. At one point he had us do an assignment where we had to write an entire paper supported by just our reasoning and argumentation skills. Furthermore, we had to spend more time making criticisms and responding to the criticsm of our own argument than we devoted to discussing it. One day after class he pulled me aside, and I assumed he was going to yell at me for being late, but instead he (much to the shock on his face) informed me that I wrote the best paper in the class (and I submitted it on time!) This experience got me to start taking a lot more philsophy classes and eventually majoring in it.

The beauty of philsophy is that it teaches you to think critically (which is way beyond stupid). For a while I thought that phrase was just another thing universities like to throw into marketing materials, but it is way more powerful than that. In business, critical thought has been the single most useful tool I have. I had no idea then—at the time I was just doing it because I thought it was fun, but now the value is huge. In business, we have to manage 10-20 or more different areas and the reality is that we are by no means expert in all of them, so as business owners we are constantly doing creative problem solving.

Since graduating from college, the learning never stopped for me. I am always absorbing new information and am continually looking to expand my knowledge base. Even though my philosophy degree was great for critical thinking, I had hardly any knowledge of business, so I created my own "personal MBA". I was at the book store 3 times a week, always scouring the business section and the personal development area for more great ideas to improve my business and my life (smart, for sure). Personally, I find it very satisfying buying physical books, reading them cover to cover and then placing them on my bookshelf as a sign of acccomplishment. When looking for books to read, I would often seek out successful entrepreneurs or business people and ask them for their favorite books. This was a great way to find the real gems out there. I also encourage my staff to do the same. Once I started hiring, training and developing people, I would encourage my team members to read certain books that I thought would help their development. I got a great reaction from that and they appreciated the time spent broadening their knowledge. Hint: we all got smarter together.

One of my favorite authors is Tim Ferris. What is unique about his approach is that he looks at ordinary business challenges and finds unconventional approaches to them. One of my favorite quotations from him is, "Our success in life can usually be determined by the number of uncomfortable conversations we're willing to have." He also discusses how the thing we most fear is what we most need to do. I thought these were brilliant points because it's easy to send out emails and fill up excel sheets, but the number one task I would often put off is making certain difficult phone calls. By looking at this quotation everyday I reminded myself how important it is to always have the tough conversations that push us forward. Additionally, I loved the concept of using fear not as something to run away from, but rather as an indicator for what needs to be done.

"There are going to be 500 Setbacks a day, but there is always another way to accomplish your goal"

Another one of my favorite authors is Richard Branson. I am a huge fan of his autobiography in a very different way than Tim Ferris. Whereas Ferris was Princeton educated and extremely methodical, Branson was much more intuitive and spontaneous. One of the many stories that blew me away was when he discussed how at age 16 he created a student newspaper. In order to get revenue, he needed to call advertisers. However, at the time he was in a strict boarding school and the headmaster denied him the use of a phone. Normally this would stop even the most motivated of us, but Branson instead came up with an ingenious way to still make the calls. He would go to the pay phone (remember those!), but he didn't have any money, so he found a loop hole. He would dial the operator and tell them that he had paid for a call but it was dropped. Everytime he did this he got an automatic free 5 minutes of talking AND the operator would even introduce him to the advertising executives, so it sounded like he had his own assistant. Little did they know!

Branson's ultimate move was to call Coca-Cola® and tell them that he had just sold Pepsi® an ad (he had not!), but the back cover was still available. In response, Pepsi booked an ad. Then, Branson actually called Coca-Cola for the first time and told them what Pepsi paid, in order to get their offer![5] What I learned from this story was to always find a way. There are going to be 500 setbacks a day but there's always another way to look at the issue and to accomplish your goal. In this case, as a 16 year old, Branson's methods were a little sneakier than I would recommend, but the spirit of his actions were sheer genius.
(And geniuses are _not_ stupid!)

Another favorite of mine is Tony Hsieh, the founder of Zappos.com. He has many fascinating stories, but one of the best recounted that after he sold his first company to Microsoft® he got a great payout at age 25. However, as part of the deal he had to let his shares vest and work at the company for another year. (Or, as he put it, "In order to vest in peace.") A few months in, however, he realized that the culture at his company had deteriorated so much that as he walked the hall of strangers he felt zero passion for what he was doing. Furthermore, his employees didn't even seem to want to be there. Despite all the success and glamor, it was empty to him. As a result, after just a few months he walked away from an eight million dollar payout. A few years later the

---

[5] Branson, Richard, Losing My Virginity, Three Rivers Press, ©1998, 2004 Richard Branson

business faltered. What I learned from this was that for both personal satisfaction and for the health of the company, you not only need to be passionate about your people, but your people need to be invested in and engaged in the company. You need a rock solid vision of what your company is and where It's going, as well as a core set of principles that you live by. The principles have to be the bedrock of your organization, and all hiring and firing decisions need to emanate from that vision and those principles.

"You need a rock solid vision of what your company is, where it's going, as well as a core set of principles to live by."

Moving forward, the next step in my personal education plan will involve covering the areas of business that are not my core strengths, or even being used today, but that I know will be essential in later stages of the business when it grows larger. At this writing, we are not a franchisor. However, we will become one in the next few years, so I am spending considerable time now researching franchise development, managing multiple locations, dealing with individual owners and all of the other future challeges we will have then. I am also actively researching and learning about different ways to get access to higher level entrepreneurs and advisors who could take us to the next level. While I am currently very knowledgable about networking, there are more sophisticated and nuanced ways to meet people in the top tier of business. In order to do so, it takes some unconventional thinking (and a little chutzpah!), but that's part of the fun. We'll call this part my "PhD in business."

Chapter XV

Know When to Go

"The Job of the Entrepreneur is to Figure Out How to Get <u>Out</u> of His Business."

—*Michael Gerber*

What's Your Exit Strategy?

One of the most familiar quotes in business is "Begin with the end in mind," popularized by Steven Covey in his book *The Seven Habits of Highly Successful People.* Michael Gerber, Author of *The E-Myth* has been quoted as saying, "The job of the entrepreneur is to get out of his business." Exit strategy isn't something to think about when you're exiting, but rather when you're starting your business. Now, when we talk about exit strategies, what we mean is not necessarily leaving the business entirely, in every case. We are asking the question of, "What does your end game look like?" Ask yourself, what's your long term plan for what you envision as a successful company, as well as what role you'd like to have in the later stages of the business? That said, let's examine several of the possible options you have for an exit strategy—whether it means less involvement in the business, or totally and completely leaving your business.

"The valuation is always the sticking point, so it's wise to have an outside qualified appraisal."

Option A: Sell to an employee. Let's look at the upside to this option first. In this case, you are transitioning the company to someone familiar with the business already; someone who is fully trained, who understands the culture. Furthermore, you don't have to go through an extensive search to find them, there's a good trust factor already (assuming you are the one who picked them) and they are an insider, so they genuinely know the strengths and weaknesses of the business. So, what's the downside of selling to an employee? Depending on whether the company is in an upswing or a downswing matters. If there's a lack of growth, or even worse, a downswing, then selling to someone already in the company might just enforce the status quo. It might also devalue it a little bit because they know too much. (Hint: the valuation is always the sticking point in all of these scenarios, so it's wise to have an outside valuation done by a qualified appraiser.)

Option B: Sell to a competitor. The obvious advantages to this option are that the buyer knows the industry already, they're likely poised for growth if they're looking for a takeover—which means that they're likely well capitalized. The flip side of this approach: if the sale falls through, then they gain information on your weaknesses. In addition, there might be a potentially adversarial relationship from a history as competitors, which could hinder the negotiation. Unless you're taking business away from them, they are probably not willing to offer the highest purchase price, and there's likely no established trust going into talks, since it's unlikely that you'd have a close relationship with them. Sometimes there are friendly competitors, but that's not often the case. Of course you'll need to make sure you have all the proper NDA's (non-disclosure agreements) signed and other protections.

Option C: Sell to a supplier. There are a few strong reasons why this may make sense. First, the acquiring company knows the industry, is most likely well capitalized compared to you and probably has more leverage in the marketplace. So, why not do this? Consider that they might leak intel on your company to a competitor. Otherwise, there are not too many downsides with this route, except that this only applies to certain industries.

Option D: Asset Sale. Obviously, you don't plan for this situation. It's one of the less desirable exit strategies— generally a last resort when you're unable to sell the whole business (often when there are substantial liabilities), but it is a backup solution that is often favorable for a distressed company. That can include hard assests like vehicles, real estate, etc. and soft assets like intellectual property, procedures manuals, etc.

Option E: Hire A CEO/Move To An emeritus role/board of directors. Another option is to exit from the day to day running of a business and instead, move to an advisory capacity, or a board of directors position, or act as a silent partner. Initially, this could be more expensive because you now have a highly paid executive. However, if that person does increase the profitability of the company, then you could increase your income and your eventual buy-out with dramatically less work and less stress.

Option F: Franchising. Franchising is another situation that is costly to set up. Most companies charge a minimum of six figures right out the gate in legal fees and there are a lot of compliance issues to be met. Those regulatory issues cannot be bypassed or it will almost always end poorly. However, when it's set up it can be a great opportunity because you have highly motivated individuals who have a lot of upside due to their ownership stake. For the various locations you can basically be hands off with the day to day. However, one of the top reasons why certain franchisees fail is a lack of support from the head office of the franchisor. On the upside, if you do franchise your business, there is the potential for residual income and global expansion. Keep in mind that not every business is franchisable. You must have proprietary systems and processes that are duplicatable and teachable.

Option G: Licensing. Similar to franchising, licensing is a play off of your intellectual property whereby you can create an income stream with ongoing residual profit while still owning the intellectual property. Celebrities frequently do this by licensing their name, their likeness, etc. to other companies' products and services. One great example is Nike® Air Jordan sneakers. Michael Jordan then gets a cut on every pair sold. With franchising the franchisor needs to take a more pro-active role in the success of the individual locations. However, with licensing there is often less obligation to do so. Ultimately, the profits can sometimes be higher for franchises than licensing, but it's important to weigh the pros and cons based on your specific sitation.

Option H: IPO. Ah yes, the lure of the stock market! Besides the glamor and the bragging rights, the upside to becoming a publicly traded company is the potentially huge cash infusion, international brand awareness and a potential for global expansion. The downsides: volatility, loss of control, potential for dilution of your shares in the company—and in a worst case scenario, getting kicked out of your own company. Beyond that, consider that you also open yourself up to potential hostile takeover, much more regulatory scrutiny, concern over shareholder value dropping in down markets and your customers and investors losing money. Finally, you have to make business decisions based on quarterly returns and market pressures instead of what's in the interest of the business or a sound long term strategy.

Business owners frequently dream of having a publicly traded company with all the recognition and the major cash infusion. Still, there are plenty of times when it's simply not a good idea. Richard Branson took his company public and then made it private later on because when the stock took a hit, he couldn't bear seeing people who trusted him to invest in the company losing their money.

Option I: Passing your business to family members. There are favorable reasons to do this, such as the trust factor, keeping it closely held in the family and protecting trade secrets from strangers. Also, you know what you're getting—good or bad—the strengths and the weaknesses you most likely already know. There's some predictability, to say the least. On the downside, the emotional attachment you have might not result in making the best decisions for the company. For example, you give it to one of your sons who then runs it into the ground; they didn't earn it so they might not share your passion and enthusiasm. Third generation family-owned businesses also have a fairly high failure rate statistically speaking. Also consider that if there are multiple family members there's room for a lot of complication and conflict. Witness high profile cases such as Viacom®, run by the Redstone family, and Newscorp, run by the Murdoch family. Even though Viacom is a publicly traded company, they have been subject to the whims of long term personal family squabbles. (Usually not smart.)

Option J: Acquisition by VC or private equity firm. There are some very viable upsides to this exit strategy. Besides the substantial cash infusion, these firms bring a great deal of expertise. And that expertise is hugely valuable because you get the high level contacts, relationships and experience of the team. They're already experienced in doing all the things that need to be done to grow your company, they can bring on experts in almost any field, they are well versed in recruitment, finances, talent acquisition, supplier relationships, etc. It's not all rosy, of course. You need to take into account the loss of control, the potential for dilution, the pressure to hit certain milestones (or they take more equity) and what can become a very cut throat environment with deadlines set by someone else. Keep in mind that very often you have to pay the due diligence fees upfront before they will even look at you. If you're less than a ten million dollar company, these firms will seldom even entertain purchasing your company.

How (and When) to Prepare for a Smooth, Profitable Exit

The first consideration is assessing when it makes sense to sell. You want to do it when your company is at its peak performance. Before anything else, make sure all your financial records are in good order. If there is any fat to trim, now is the time to drop excess inventory, any "dead wood" (looking at you, Janice in HR!) Time for uncle Mo to retire! Now is the time to line up all the right consultants—an appraiser for your valuation, a good business attorney (not your brother-in-law's kid who just graduated law school), an accountant and other outside professionals (not your internal controller), potentially a franchise consultant if that applies.

When valuing a business, you will typically use the EBIT formula, which is Earnings Before Interest and Taxes. You calculate this as 3-5 times your yearly net profit. Many other factors come into play for the final valuation, such as soft assets like intellecual property (patents and trade secrets). However, this is a good rule of thumb to get a quick ball park idea of what your business should sell for. Monitor the recent sales of companies similar to your own to get a feel for the value.

It is essential to keep in mind that any business that is totally dependent on its owner is virtually worthless. When someone is purchasing a business they are looking to take it over without losing the income coming into the business. If the owner still brings in half the company's accounts, then unless the owner agrees to stay on for a very long time, the company is vastly less attractive and arguably not sellable.

It's a matter of looking at all of the assets and the liabilities of the company. You need to maximize the assets and minimize the liabilities. How can you achieve this? Start by closing down any and all unprofitable lines of business. You want the P&L (profit and loss statement) to look as strong as possible. If you have certain products or services that don't add much to the bottom line, they need to be cut. By doing so, you will also be able to cut staff and other equipment expenses that those products and services require. This process is key to becoming lean, yet profitable. Expect the aquiring entity to hold you to some kind of non-compete agreement for at least a period of time. It's fair and it makes good business sense for them. That said, after that period it's totally possible to go back into your previous industry, so make sure that the non-compete is not too onerous. (That would be stupid, for sure.)

With your employees, you need to figure out who would be staying on. First there's the matter of deciding when to bring it up with key staff and when to tell the whole company. And when you do, it's key to make it clear to them that it's in their best interest to stay on – if they are a key asset to the business. So you need to determine an attractive succession plan and one that serves not just you, but also the people who helped get you there, to benefit and profit from the sale. At certain times, some acquiring entities might not be aligned with this philosophy and will want to gut the company. Try to understand the acquiring entity's plans and make sure you're okay with them. Or, if they do decide to bring in their people, then it's best to offer your key staff part of the payout or an exit package. Of course, don't promise anything you can't deliver.

Conclusion

"Success is the Ability to Go From One Failure to Another With No Loss of Enthusiasm."

—*Winston Churchill*

It has been said that the one constant is change, and no matter what plan you devise—plan on changing it. Our own real world, in the trenches experience has taught us that flexibility is king. It's paramount to your success. The other thing we learned is that the only stupid idea is the one that you don't pursue. If you really believe in it, then test it, kick sand at it, throw it against the wall—but DO IT if it makes sense after all that. Remember: Be different, try crazy stuff; don't do the conventional; stand up, stand out, get noticed. Be distruptive—market and advertise so that you can see heads turning from a mile away. Don't follow the trends now—predict where they are going and get there first.

If you take anything away from this book, make sure it's this: the idea of experimenting, testing and measuring— then executing. We can't stress enough the importance of good planning—but, equally important is the ability to adjust, change, flex and respond. Remember, do not go it alone—surround yourself with great people and build out a team. It's all about getting the right people in the right seats. Hire people who build you and your company up every day and do the exact same to them in return. Surround yourself with the greatest people you can find and never stop looking for them or be content with "just okay."

Use your intuition when you know something is right, but at the same time find others who know more than you and lean on them as much as possible. Build a culture based on rock solid core values that will make people thrilled to be a part of your organization because everyone is beating the same drum. The old management style is out. The days of the referee, priest, or dictator are over. Manage like a diplomat.

On another note, remember the importance of lifelong learning and above all, the importance of carving out your own path – following the beat of a different drummer. Remain a leader, not a follower. The world has enough flocks of sheep. As you chase your dream and build your business, learn the rules and regulations very well—and then figure out which ones to break. Live within your financial means and never push the limits too far. Aim for hypergrowth; scale fast – be growth oriented; set aggressive time tables.

Never forget: it all comes down to people—the customers, the suppliers, the employees, the managers—it's all about people. If you don't develop top notch people skills, you'll never succeed.

Looking to the future, my cloudy crystal ball says if you build a business and follow these principles, there's a good chance you won't end up like previous generations, getting knocked down the corporate ladder or kicked to the curb. Once you have everything all together, then base everything around rock solid systems that will make life easier and automated and a breeze to manage. Do all these things and you will experience business hypergrowth more than you could even imagine. You can and must *always find a way.* It's the entrepreneur's creed or mantra—because there's no backup; there's no "can't"—there's only "won't." It's the idea of never taking a "no". You're always continually adjusting things and figuring it out, because there's no other option.

Always remember this core tenet of youthpreneurship, what Seth Godin termed "Permission Marketing" –it's a major paradigm shift. We are in the era where the consumer is in charge. He or she has already shopped and knows what they want; your job: to make it easy for them to buy. Information is all they need. And nearly any information the consumer could want is online! There are stars and ratings – so much great feedback. Websites, blogs, newsletters all show the consumer great reviews. That's the kind of bedrock that allowed us to grow our own business quickly. Do right by the customer and they will become your best spokesperson. Mess up and they will tell the world about it. Your choice. (Like we haven't said it enough, let's not be stupid.)

That's one of the widely held criticisms of our generation— the notion of entitlement. You can choose and follow your own path, but you still gotta earn it, baby!

One of my favorite quotes is from playwright Samuel Beckett, which is, "Ever tried. Ever failed. No matter. Try

Again. Fail again. Fail better." That's the central idea of this book. How do we fail better? I realize I'm basically telling you to find new ways to screw up more, but I'm okay with that. Make no mistake that screwing up is the key to success—and the path to business hypergrowth. Because the more mistakes you learn from means the more actions you are taking. And each new bold action into the unknown, the unfamiliar and the uncomfortable pushes you one step closer to your ultimate goal— whatever it may be for you.

When all is said and done, here's what distinguishes our generation from others: we're not working for retirement anymore. We don't want to slave away to get the pot of gold at the end of the rainbow, hating our careers just to save money and then START enjoying life at retirement time. We are the "journey is the destination" generation. Enjoy THAT! We think it's a smarter path.

You have to be stupid enough to quit your job...
Stupid enough to take a chance on your idea...
Stupid enough to take the right calculated risks...
Stupid enough to do whatever it takes...
Stupid enough to be an entrepreneur...
And if you are, you might just be stupid enough to succeed.

—*Jeff Naeem*

About the Author

Destined for entrepreneurship at an early age, Jeff Naeem sold wrapping paper door-to-door at the ripe old age of seven. While still in school, he became one of the top 100 sales performers in the country for Cutco knives. He earned a concentration in philosophy at Hamilton College.

After college, fear of living in a box drove him to take a job in financial services. After growing weary of the 9-5 grind, at the suggestion of a friend, he decided to hang up the suit and tie and become a full time junk guy. He likes to say he traded in junk bonds for junk removal and he loves what he does. Jeff started doing the hauling himself but now his company Junk-A-Haulics® has a fleet of trucks, multiple locations, a team of clean cut professional haulers and a growing brand ripe for franchising. The company became profitable in just three months and has grown 50-75% each year. As he continues to expand in the New Jersey market he plans on eventually offering franchises to likeminded entrepreneurs who want to grow his brand, which his tagline best sums up as "The Professionals In A Dirty Business."

Jeff has spoken before local and regional business organizations and has been interviewed on Jim Beach's "School for Startups" syndicated radio show, featured in *New Jersey Business* magazine, The "Daily Record", has guest blogged for the worldwide Entrepreneurs' Organization and is on the Board of the EO Accelerator. He has also appeared as a workshop presenter for the Next Level Conference, sponsored by the Institute for Entrepreneurial Leadership.

When Jeff isn't running his business, he is either hiking and enjoying other outdoor activities, live music or sampling craft beer.